D1541551

YES I CAN!

Stand Up to Life's Put-downs

YES I CAN!

Stand Up to Life's Put-downs

Kenneth J. Brown

© 2004 by Kenneth J. Brown

ISBN: 0-97559573-0

Timely Timeless Books, LLC
Columbus, OH
1-866-669-4047

Books Designed to Help You Live Long and Prosper

www.TimelessBooks.net

Cover Design by S. Beckman Print & Graphic Solutions, Inc.

Printed and bound in the United States of America.

Dedication

YES I CAN! is dedicated to you. Yes, *you!*
Your potential, *your* future, and *your* success.
You can do it! This book will show *you* the way.

Acknowledgements

In his *Biography for Beginners*, E.C. Bentley jotted this clever little diddy:

> **The Art of Biography**
> **Is different from Geography.**
> **Geography is about Maps,**
> **But Biography is about Chaps.**

I owe a debt of gratitude to the "Chaps"—both men and women—whose stories fill the pages of YES I CAN! It is because of their courage, resolution, and determination that these true stories are worth telling. It is because these "chaps" were or *are* living, breathing, daring human "becomings" that these are not tall tales. They are true stories that have inspired my own "story." I hope they will change or enhance your "story" too.

When all is said and done, I hope that there isn't more said than done. I trust that you will wrap these stories in shoe leather and discover that you aren't just a human being. You are a human "becoming," someone with tremendous God-given potential. You are not limited by what the "experts" or your critics have told you can do or be. You are limited only if you are willing to believe them and be restrained by their sorry advice or their endless criticism.

Sure, you have endured your unfair share of verbal slaps and put-downs. But take notice how the men and women in these stories refused to stay down when they were put-down. Watch how they stood up to their critics and determine to imitate their example. As you follow in their footsteps, you will discover that you have recovered your footing and that you are following your dreams and ambitions once more.

Here is what I suspect you will find. When you have finished reading these wonderful stories, you will discover that you owe a debt of gratitude to these "Chaps" too. It is a debt that you will never be able to pay back, but you can always pay it forward.

—Kenneth J. Brown
July, 2004

Preface

What challenges are you facing in your life?

What changes do you need to make in your life?

What would you do differently, if you had the courage to try—or try again?

If you need to take on new challenges in your life, these intriguing stories in YES I CAN! will motivate you to tackle those challenges head first.

If you need to make changes in your life, these stories will supply you with a courage transfusion to do whatever you need to do.

If you need to get back up after getting knocked down or put-down, these stories will help you find your feet again.

Sit back, relax, put your feet up, and enjoy several great stories. Or read 'em all at once! Read them aloud to your spouse . . . or your kids . . . or your friends. See these stories through their eyes and share the lessons you learn with the people you love.

But be prepared! Once you put this book down, you will have to get up and get moving. You have critics to set straight and "experts" to prove wrong. Whatever you do, have fun putting them in their place.

Table of Contents

Why Go Forward?
An Introduction

"You will love these stories!"

Sure! Every author would stake that claim, wouldn't they? But you, as the reader, reserve the right to ask, "Why would I like this book?" Or, "Why would I find these stories engaging?" Or even, "What does this book offer me that I won't find anywhere else?"

Those are excellent questions. Relevant questions. Sensational questions! They deserve top-notch answers. I will do my best to give you a first-rate response.

Let me try answering your questions by asking you a couple of questions in return? Have you ever had someone pour cold water on your red-hot ideas? Or have you ever been the victim of one or more of these common put-downs?

- **"You will never amount to anything!"**
- **"You can't do that!"**
- **"You will never succeed at anything you ever do!"**
- **"You don't look the part!"**
- **"Your idea will never fly!"**
- **"You are doomed to fail!"**
- **"You aren't smart enough to do what you want to do!"**
- **"You can't! Nobody else has ever been able to do it!"**
- **"You don't know anything!"**
- **"You don't have the talent to achieve your dream!"**
- **"You fool! That's a dumb idea!"**

7

If you've faced these put-downs, or their kissin' cousins (and who hasn't), then **this book is for you!** The stories in this book are relevant to where you live, and to what you must live down. Each story features somebody who had to stand up to one of these garden variety put-downs.

But the heroes and heroines of these stories succeeded at the very task or goal others predicted they could never achieve. Each of these somebodies is *Somebody* because he or she dared to stand up to life's put-downs. These stories will inspire you to stand up to those who sit in judgment of you.

Teddy Roosevelt was right! America's famed "Rough Rider," the 26th President of the United States, knew how to stand up to his detractors:

> "It is not the critic who counts: not the man who points out how the strong man stumbled or where the doer of the deeds could have done them better. The credit belongs to the man who is actually in the arena; whose face is marred by dust and sweat and blood; who strives valiantly; who errs, and comes short again and again, because there is not effort without error and shortcoming; who does actually try to do the deed; who knows the great enthusiasm, the great devotion, and spends himself in a worthy cause; who, at the worst, if he fails, at least fails while daring greatly. Far better it is to dare mighty things, to win glorious triumphs even though checkered by failure, than to rank with those poor spirits who neither enjoy nor suffer much because they live in the gray twilight that knows neither victory nor defeat."

Did you know that Walter Payton, the star running back of the Chicago Bears, ran just nine miles during his illustrious pro football career? But he did it while getting knocked down every 4.6

yards. He ran a grand total of 15,800 yards, but every 4.6 yards meant another punishing tackle. That's why Payton was a shoo-in to the Football Hall of Fame.

You can stand up to life's put-downs. You can't avoid them, but you can void them . . . by your success and persistence. Getting knocked down in life is a universal experience. Often to be repeated. But getting back up again—and again, if need be—is the feat of life's winners.

You can do it, too! These stories will show you how, and they will motivate you to do what many others have done. Each story concludes with a maxim designed to apply the lesson you gleaned from someone else's experience. Each maxim is preceded by a graphic like the one below, reminding you to:

Stand Up to Them!

Stand up to your critics! You can do it! Stand up to those who sit in judgment of you! You can and you must! Stand up to life's put-downs! Yes, you can! Let me hear you say it:

"Yes I Can!"

They say, "Practice makes perfect!" Practice reciting, "Yes I Can!" after you read each story in this book. By the time you are half-way through, you will be convinced that you can stand up to life's put-downs . . . and you will!

April Fools!

You know you've arrived when you land that one job you always dreamed of having, right? Then why was this young TV news anchor finding it so difficult to enjoy being, as she put it, "Ms. Broadcast Journalist?"

It was a daily struggle for her to stay emotionally detached when she covered a tragic news story. And she couldn't say the word *Canada*. How could anyone mispronounce *Canada*?

On April Fool's Day, she got the axe. It fell to the assistant news director to drop the bombshell. She was demoted and his critique was devastating. "You don't have a face for T.V.!" would be the short-hand version of what he told her:

"Your hair's too thick. Your eyes are too far apart. Your nose is too wide. Your chin is too long. You have to do something about it."

Who was he kidding? She was a former Miss Tennessee. She had won beauty contests. Besides, why did the station hire her in the first place if they had problems with her appearance on-camera? She was devastated, but the station manager offered to send her to New York for a makeover.

Against her better judgment, she went. At a salon they gave her a French perm. It burned her scalp. Her hair pulled out in clumps. One week later she was, "as bald as the great American eagle!"

Now she was a former anchorwoman with no hair who was unable to wear a wig. As she recalls, "There were no wigs big enough for my head—it's twenty-four inches around—so I had to walk around wearing scarves for months." In the meantime, the TV station sent her to a voice coach to improve her communication skills. When she returned she still had a job at the station. But doing what?

"What about co-hosting a local morning talk show?" management suggested. They were desperate to find a niche for her. And they did. Her new show was a huge hit.

Next came the move to Chicago. Before long she was hosting *A.M. Chicago*, up against the *Phil Donahue Show*, day-time T.V.'s powerhouse. People warned her that taking on Donahue was a lost cause. "They said I was black, female, and overweight."

But they were wrong. She earned the right to host her own show. To say it was successful would be a gross understatement. Her talk show's success enabled her to form her own production company, *Harpo* (which happens to be Oprah spelled backwards). And you already know the rest of that story.

Stand Up to Them!

You have what it takes if you can ignore those who say, "You don't have what it takes!"

Kind Words That Wound

Her stepfather failed to live up to his name. His name was Kind. He was not. He told his step-daughter that she was not pretty, and that she would never amount to much. When he compared her with his own daughter, he referred to them as:

"the beauty and the beast."

He made it crystal clear that her baby step-sister was the beauty and she was the ugly beast. Once, when she asked for an ice cream cone, he told her "No! You're too ugly." His put-downs were dispensed in daily doses.

She yearned to look like her movie idol, Shirley Temple. But her hair hung down, limp and straight. Her eyes were crossed, her nose was odd, and her mouth was big.

She was too ugly to live, or so she thought. Like in a surreal Cinderella fantasy, she was forced to wash the floors and do all of the chores around home. The walls of the family's apartment were her prison, and she dreamed of ways to escape from it.

Reading about cancer, she convinced herself that she had six months to live. "I'll show them," she thought. "I'll die a tragic death and then they'll be sorry." Sitting on the roof of her apartment building this petite 9-year-old girl took a puff on a cigarette and plotted her death.

But she did not die. She survived—by dreaming of becoming the greatest, the biggest and the best. "I remember a long time ago, when I was a kid, I hadda be somebody," she recalled years later. "I hadda be great. I couldn't be medium."

She isn't medium. She's larger than life!! She became a great singer, had stunning success on Broadway by the time she was 21-years-old and developed into a major film talent, both on-screen and behind the camera. But the old fears still dog her steps.

Her name and her face bring her instant recognition in public. But she hates the attention. She doesn't even enjoy singing in public, although audiences love her and applaud her performances. She has become, as one of her friends put it, "one of the great introverts of our time."

She still pays the price for a man named Kind, who was not. One song you will never hear Barbara Streisand sing is,

"Sticks and stones will break my bones,
but words will never hurt me."

Stand Up to Them!

Rise above unkind remarks.
Don't let them keep you down.

Milking It For All He Could Get

Ray was a milk shake machine salesman and this restaurant had eight Multimixer machines. It was a match made in malted heaven. He made a sales pitch to the two brothers who owned the little drive-in establishment:

> **"I've been in the kitchens of a lot of restaurants and drive-ins selling Multimixers around the country and I have never seen anything to equal the potential of this place of yours. Why don't you open a series of units like this? It would be a gold mine for you and for me, too, because every one would boost my Multimixer sales. What d'you say?"**

The brothers sat there, speechless. Then one of them turned and pointed to the house on top of the hill overlooking the restaurant. "See that big white house with the wide front porch?" he asked. "That's our home, and we love it. We sit out on the porch in the evenings and watch the sunset and look down on our place here. It's peaceful. We don't need any more problems. We are in a position to enjoy life now, and that's just what we intend to do."

His brother agreed. "It'll be a lot of trouble." They didn't need the hassle.

Their complacency stunned the ambitious milk shake machine salesman. He envisioned these little drive-ins multiplying like rabbits. If he could find a way to reproduce them, he could get rich selling Multimixers. There was a fortune to be made in shakes and he wanted to milk it for all he could get.

He convinced the brothers to sell him the rights to franchise their drive-in restaurant. Visions of milk shakes danced in his head. However, once the drive-ins started to dot the landscape, Ray realized that Multimixers weren't the real goldmine. These little restaurant franchises were the key to his fortune.

The drive-ins were modeled after the McDonald brothers' restaurant in San Bernadino, California. With their golden arches and golden-brown French fries, they are everywhere you want to be. More than 12,000 franchises worldwide.

Believe it or not, *McDonald's* golden arches are, according to *Extra* (the T.V. show), more recognizable as a symbol around the world than the cross of Christ!

Can you imagine Ray Kroc dreaming of Multimixer sales when he had an agreement to franchise *McDonald's* in his briefcase? What a crock!

Stand Up to Them!

**Your vision can be a little short-sighted,
if it is big enough for the long haul.**

One Man's "Can't!"
Is Another Man's "Can!"

Vernon Johns knew his time had come. He stepped up to take the lead. But no one followed. He challenged others who were treated with indiginity to follow his example. Nobody did! He shook his head in disgust and later told a friend:

**"Even God can't free people
who behave like that."**

Vernon, a local pastor, gave his church a black eye. He was a stubborn man who refused to leave after he had left. He resigned from the church, but refused to leave the parsonage. In frustration, the church leaders had the gas, electricity and water disconnected. Vernon didn't budge. He read by candlelight, carried his own water and kept warm by burning old newspapers. This "siege" lasted more than a year. By the time Vernon vacated the parsonage, the members of the church were embarrassed and bitter.

A recent graduate with a Ph.D. interviewed to take Vernon's place as the pastor of the church. Friends warned the young man that he was walking into a hornet's nest. This church had a reputation for being difficult. "They chew up their pastors, and spit them out," they said.

His father, a successful pastor in his own right, warned him not to go to that church. But, like many energetic young men have done before him, he ignored the advice. He was up to the challenge.

There were obstacles to overcome, but the promising young pastor had established a strong following. He became a leader in his church and then a leader in his community. In a short time, he even assumed a leadership role on the national stage.

His influence in the community escalated when he convinced people who felt mistreated, to boycott the local buses. His predecessor, Vernon Johns, had failed to convince one bus load of blacks to take seats in the front of the bus. But this young Ph.D. convinced multitudes to boycott every bus in the city to protest various indignities all of them had endured.

It was a remarkable strategy, and the success of the boycott drew attention from *Time* magazine and *The New York Times*. This young pastor was thrust into a role as the conscience of the nation. Years later, he urged black Americans to pile onto buses for a trip to the nation's capitol. His "March on Washington" drew more than 250,000 "marchers." They gathered peacefully in the name of freedom.

Vernon Johns failed to see how God could set these people free. But Dr. Martin Luther King, Jr. saw that God could and would. He convinced his fellow Americans to believe it, too. His majestic words ring true today, almost forty years later.

"Free at last! Free at last!
Thank God Almighty, we're free at last!"

Stand Up to Them!

Don't conclude, "It can't be done!" or someone else will have to do it for you.

Not A Chance!

Literary agents must dread hearing, "This book could be a best-seller!" One author dared to dream that his book would be popular enough to be sold in airport bookstores. His agent set him straight. "You are no Jeffrey Archer," the man predicted, referring to a best-selling British fiction writer.

"He told me there was no chance of that. It might sell well to academics and students, but a book like that couldn't break into Jeffrey Archer territory."

Surprise! The book was on *The New York Times* best-seller list for 53 weeks. Across "the pond" it lasted 184 weeks on *The Sunday Times* of London list before it made *The Guinness Book of Records*. No other book had ever made that many appearances on the London *Times* list. It has since been translated into a minimum of 33 languages.

No one imagined the book would be so successful. Not even the author. His ambitions were bush league. When he wrote it, he was hoping to be able to use the royalties to *help* pay for his daughter's college tuition.

How appropriate that the book was released on April Fool's Day. Everyone was fooled by its success. More than 5.5 million copies have been sold worldwide at last count. As the author, a noted mathematician, commented, "That is about one copy for every nine hundred and seventy men, women, and children in the world."

How do the experts and critics explain the book's success now? Some say that, "People buy the book but don't actually read it, far less understand it." Then, as if to add insult to injury, the critics gripe that people, "just want to be seen with the book or that owning it gives them the comfortable feeling that they are in possession of knowledge, without their having to go to the effort of reading it."

Aside from the intellectual hurdle that his critics recognized, the author had to overcome some incredible personal odds. Not long after he accepted the offer from the publisher, he contracted pneumonia. His doctors performed a tracheotomy, which left him speechless, *literally*.

Trapped in a wheel chair by ALS (Lou Gehrig's disease), he could not write. Now he was unable to talk. How could he hope to put his thoughts on paper? Initially, he communicated at a snail's pace. Someone would point to a letter on a flash card and he would raise his eyebrows to indicate, "Yes, use that letter." Every word was a major achievement.

A computer programmer in California heard about his plight and sent him a specialized software program. It allowed the budding author to choose whole words from a series of menus on screen by pressing a switch in his hand. Or he could operate the program by a special switch controlled by certain head or eye movements. Using this method, he managed to "write" fifteen words a minute.

When the book was eventually published, it was an overnight success. Six months after it was released someone decided to make a film of the book. That led to a companion volume that the author joked was, "The Book of The Film of The Book."

When you stop to think about it, it is hard to believe that a book on physics could enjoy such extraordinary success. Nobody in their right mind imagined that a technical discussion of black holes, quantum mechanics, antiparticles, imaginary time, naked singularities and special relativity would sell two dozen copies. Except to other physicists. Yet this book invaded "Jeffrey Archer territory" and conquered its farthest frontiers.

So, if this brief history of Stephen Hawking's *A Brief History of Time* serves any purpose, it reminds you to take a chance when the "experts" say that there is "no chance."

Stand Up to Them!

You must chart a new course when your critics tell you, "You can't get there from here!"

An "Out of This World" Success

Don't you just love movie critics? Actually, don't you often love the movies that film critics hate? A case in point: one movie critic grumbled that a particular "kiddie" film was . . .

**"the worst film I have ever seen . . .
nauseating, sentimental rubbish."**

Ah, but there was one small glitch. Audiences loved it! They flooded the theaters, parents bringing their kids and kids dragging their parents. This "nauseating" film was more than just a box-office smash. It grossed $700 million! More than any movie ever had or ever would—until the same director scored an even bigger hit with more spectacular creatures.

It was a simple story portraying the love of a 10-year-old boy for a polyurethane alien branded *E.T.* This "sentimental rubbish" slammed Steven Spielberg into hyper-drive on his way to becoming the most successful movie director in the galaxy.

Stand Up to Them!

**Your critics don't matter much.
Your fans matter most!**

Fired, But Not Finished

A young actress was fired by Columbia Pictures after her first movie role. A composite of the studio's comments about her were very revealing:

"Can't act," "Voice like a tight squeak," "Utterly unsure of herself," and "Unable even to take refuge in her own insignificance."

No doubt they could have added something trite like, "She'll never work in this town again!" But they would be wrong. Her tight, squeaky voice became her trademark. She found "refuge" in serving as the world's most enduring sex symbol.

"If I have to be a symbol of something," she told *Life* magazine, "I'd rather have it be sex than anything else." That interview appeared in *Life*'s August 3, 1962 issue. One night later she was discovered in her bedroom, dead from an apparent suicide.

She has been dead for more than 40 years. But her image thrives because of many memorable movie roles and a slew of priceless photos. A film studio's verdict on Marilyn Monroe's "insignificance" seems utterly insignificant . . . and completely ridiculous today.

Stand Up to Them!

**"Insignificance" becomes less significant
as you achieve greater significance.**

A Ripping Good Tale

John Hunt, in the early 19th century, thought he knew what he was talking about when he drew this comparison between an Englishman and one of those "foreign" artists:

> **"He is not to be compared in the painting of character with our extraordinarily gifted English artist Mr. Rippingille."**

What a pitiful comparison! Mr. Rippingille's name and reputation might be meaningful to a few select art critics and historians, but he is not someone whose name opens wallets or doors to art galleries.

Yet, the "foreign" painter that Mr. Hunt judged to be inferior is considered one of the world's greatest painters. Some would argue that he is the greatest. One described him as, "Shakespeare with a paintbrush and pallette." He was a master at capturing "character" on canvas.

Have you ever heard of the "extraordinarily gifted" Mr. Rippingille? Do you have any idea how much a painting by this English artist is worth in today's market? Perhaps a couple thousand dollars for one of his most distinguished works.

By comparison, one painting by this lowly "foreign" artist could empty a Swiss bank account. Even his etchings and sketches are worth infinitely more than a painting by the "extraordinarily gifted English artist."

Consider these examples: In early 1995, two of the "foreign" artist's paintings were purchased by the Getty Museum for an estimated $35 million. Later, in December of that same year, a collector paid Sotheby's auction house in London $5,320,000 for one of the "foreign" artist's other lesser known works, "Cupid Blowing a Soap Bubble."

In early 1997, an anonymous telephone bidder bought "the most expensive painting per square inch" from Southeby's. This miniature collectible, a 4 1/8" by 2 3/4" portrait of an old man with a beard, sold for $2.9 million. That's $272,941 per square inch! But who's counting?

You may not recognize the name Rippingille. But you can't help but know Rembrandt's name! Can you?

Stand Up to Them!

Who do "they" always compare you with?
Are you sure "they" are right?

One Is Better Than Two

David O. Selznick of RKO Studio ordered a screen test for an aspiring actor, "in spite of his enormous ears and bad chin line." Another studio exec concluded:

**"Can't act. Can't sing.
Balding. Can dance a little."**

Theatre critics were not impressed by his solo appearances either. They were used to seeing him on-stage with his glamorous sister. One carped, "He stops every now and then to look off-stage towards the wings as if he were hoping his titled sister, Adele, would come out and rescue him."

Another complained, "One thing is certain. After viewing last night's performance we have come to the conclusion that two . . . are better than one."

Burns Mantle, in the *New York Mirror*, was even less kind, if that was possible. "Of course, you never would pick him out of any line-up to play a romantic hero, with or without music. He hasn't the hair for one thing."

Enormous ears, a bad chin line, thinning hair and a face "the shape of an upside-down Bartlett pear," another Broadway critic sneered. Not great qualifications for a leading man on stage or in films, do you think? Without his sister by his side, many thought his career was in the tank. In Boston, the *Transcript* noted that it is "not for the general good" that he is "now sisterless."

But he was destined to remain "sisterless." His sister had quit the stage to become Lady Cavendish, marrying an English nobleman. Meanwhile, Hollywood paired "sisterless" with another young dancer who had thirteen films to her credit. Their names are now synonymous with dance. He and Ginger Rogers danced their way into the hearts of audiences all around the world.

Despite the carping of the critics, "sisterless" did sing. And he appeared in a host of hit movies. A Hollywood "walk-of-fame" sensation despite his big ears, bad chin, and thinning hair.

For somebody who could only "dance a little," Fred Astaire sure did dance a lot!

Stand Up to Them!

Why did you conclude, "I can't!"?
Oh, because somebody said, "You can't!"
What if that person is dead wrong?

A Swing And A Miss-take

Baseball great Tris Speaker, a Hall of Fame slugger in his own right, blew this call:

> **"He made a big mistake**
> **when he gave up pitching."**

It was Tris Speaker who made the "big mistake" in 1921. That same year the ex-pitcher slugged 59 home runs. Six years later, at age 32, he belted 60 home runs!

Granted, he did strike out 1,330 times during his major league career. But most people don't think of strikeouts when they think of Babe Ruth. They picture those dramatic home runs. His 714 "round-trippers" set a record that stood for more than 40 years.

Stand Up to Them!

Who has told you that you made a "big mistake?"
I wonder, "Could he or she have been mistaken?"

Him, a Success? Ha!

He did not learn to speak at a normal age. When he was nine years old, he was still not fluent in his native tongue. He was seven before he learned to read. If a teacher asked the boy a question, it took him forever to respond.

So you wouldn't be surprised to learn that his principal had low expectations regarding the boy's future, would you? When his father asked what profession the young man should consider, the headmaster replied,

> **"It doesn't matter, he'll never make a success of anything."**

That was, undoubtedly, the biggest miscalculation that the headmaster ever made. This boy, whose early development was retarded in significant ways, matured into *the* scientific genius of his generation. Maybe of any generation.

It was a Munich headmaster who made the mistake of telling Hermann Einstein that his son would never amount to much. Young Albert started out slow, but finished with a very quick mind.

Stand Up to Them!

Those who predict that you won't amount to much have probably never amounted to much.

A Good Story About
A Great Story

Hatty did not expect to make any money from her book. It had appeared in serial form in the *National Era* for nearly a year before it arrived in bookstores. Each month's chapter ended in a nail-biting climax, enticing readers to look forward to the next selection. But most people interested in the subject of her book had already had a chance to read it in these monthly editions. Her publisher, John P. Jewett, warned her not to expect a great response to it.

> **He told her that the subject she had chosen
> was unpopular and commented that she took
> far too long to tell the story.**

It was published as a two-volume set. How many people could be expected to buy, let alone read, a two-volume novel in the mid-nineteenth century? Neither Hatty nor her publisher expected much of a response.

The publisher, hoping to minimize his risk, offered her a 50-50 split on the profit or loss from the book sales. Unfortunately, on the advice of a friend (who hadn't read the manuscript), Hatty chose plan B. She received a 10 percent royalty on every copy sold in the U.S.

To everyone's surprise, the book made publishing history in its very first week on the shelves. During that week, it sold 10,000 copies. To keep up with the demand, the publisher had to run three presses 24 hours a day. After its first year on the market, the book had sold more than 300,000 copies.

In England, sales were even more brisk. Hatty did not have a copyright in Britain and received no royalties on sales there. But after one year, the book had sold a million and a half copies in

England. But that was not the end of the story. Her book was translated into 37 different languages.

Poet John Greenleaf Whittier dropped her a note to say, "Ten thousand thanks for thy immortal book." Another poet, Henry Wadsworth Longfellow, sent Hatty a letter full of very high praise for her book. "It is one of the greatest triumphs recorded in literary history, to say nothing of the higher triumph of its moral effect."

Charles Dickens wrote to express his admiration for her literary triumph. "I have read your book with the deepest interest and sympathy, and admire, more than I can express to you, both the generous feeling which inspired it, and the admirable power with which it is executed."

As a final tribute to her work, the book was adapted for the stage. It became one of the most popular plays in its day. Maybe of all time.

But newspapers in the south denounced her book as "a pack of lies." A book review in the *Southern Quarterly Review* called it, "the loathsome rakings of a foul fancy." Claiming the book was filled with falsehoods, the *Atlanta Planter* lampooned Hatty as the "wicked authoress."

Another paper, the *Southern Literary Messenger*, attacked her as a "vile wretch in petticoats." Also, the *New Orleans Crescent* lashed out at her work. "There never before was anything so detestable or so monstrous among women as this," it editorialized.

Hatty's novel stirred up a ton of intense emotion. Someone, distressed by the graphic details about slavery in her book, sent her a package containing the severed ear of a slave.

In 1862, during the Civil War, Abraham Lincoln was introduced to Harriet Beecher Stowe for the first time. Her book had been in print for a decade by then. Hatty was greeted by the President with words that must have made her wince: "So you're the little woman that wrote the book that made this great war!"

Ah, yes! *Uncle Tom's Cabin* was more explosive than anybody, including the author and the publisher, ever imagined.

Stand Up to Them!

When other people try to lower your expectations make sure that you raise the question, "Why?"

Speechless in England

Only the "dunces" at Harrow School, in the outskirts of London, were taught English. Latin and Greek were reserved for the boys with the brightest minds. It was common practice to confine the most stupid boys to learning English exclusively. Reflecting that kind of harsh judgment, a speech teacher at Harrow wrote on one 16 year old's report card,

"A conspicuous lack of success."

How would you like to be known as the speech teacher who predicted that Winston Churchill did not have a promising future as a public speaker? By the sheer force of his rhetoric, Churchill inspired England to weather Hitler's "blitzkrieg."

Any other prime minister might have been content to congratulate the R.A.F. with blasé words like: "My, you really have to hand it to the Air Force, don't you?"

Not Churchill. He expressed his gratitude with these unforgettable phrases:

"Never in the field of human conflict
was so much owed by so many to so few."

Stand Up to Them!

**How do you know you can't be successful?
Oh . . . somebody told you that, too!**

"They'll Never Sell!"

Alexander Dow, the head honcho at the Edison Illuminating Company, gave his enterprising employee what he thought was great advice:

> **"Electricity, yes, there's the coming thing. But gas—no."**

Dow offered the young man a promotion. He could become a general superintendent at Edison. There was only one condition: this skilled mechanic would have to give up his experiments and turn his attention to more "useful" work. Meaning electricity.

This ultimatum didn't sit well with the ambitious mechanic. He quit his job with the utility company to serve as the chief engineer and a business partner in a new company focused on this new energy source: gasoline.

But, in a matter of months, he grew disillusioned by the grating expectations of his business partners. They saw only dollar signs. He saw signs of the changes needed in design and assembly. Nine months after the birth of the new company, he quit, and the company died.

To save money, he and his wife moved in with his father. It was not an easy move. His dad was skeptical of his son's experiments and saw no future in the machines that his son hoped to build. He predicted:

> **"You'll never make a go of it.
> They'll never sell."**

His father never made a worse judgment call.

A year after the failure of the first company, the son was back in business with a new group of investors. But the new company was doomed to a crib death. He and his new partners couldn't see eye-to-eye, either. These "parasites," as he referred to them, wanted production. He wanted perfection. After less than four months with the new company he quit, walking away with $900 and the blueprints for his vaunted "999."

By building and showing off his "999," he attracted the attention of another local businessman, Alexander Malcomson. With Malcomson as the chief investor, they started another company.

But it was not easy to attract other investors. When Malcomson approached a local banker, the man snorted, "Invest in a horseless carriage? Asinine folly." Twisting his friend's arm, Malcomson replied, "Put up some money, and I'll guarantee it anytime within a year."

Fortunately for his heirs, the banker accepted the risk. His $10,500 investment netted his estate more than $27 million thirteen years later. Plus the millions of dollars they made on stock dividends.

Poor Malcomson. He cashed out after three years, selling his 255 shares in the company for $175,000. If he had held out for ten more years his settlement would have been worth $64 million, according to the buyout formula.

As you can tell, the new company was very successful. Drawing on the ingenuity of the skilled mechanic with a seventh-grade education, the company launched its first "horseless carriage" in 1903.

Henry Ford, whose father told him, "They'll never sell," sold 1,700 of his first model of gas-powered vehicles, the Model A. Twelve years later, in 1915, Ford drove his one millionth car off the assembly line. By the end of the 1930s, the company had produced 28 million cars.

Unfortunately, his father never lived to see Henry "make a go of it." Not long after the Ford Motor Company started, Henry's father died. Many years later, near the end of his own life, Ford confessed to a friend, "There's just one thing I regret. I wish my father could have lived to see what happened." In fact, his father didn't live long enough to see Henry and his family move out again.

Ford's credo was, "I will build a motorcar for the multitudes." Since the "horseless carriage" was considered a luxury for the idle rich, the very notion of farmers and shop girls owning one was ridiculous. Old J.P. Morgan's bank, the House of Morgan, told him to keep such daydreams to himself.

When Ford announced that he would double the wages of his employees to $5 a day, the publisher of *The New York Times* was overheard to say, "He's crazy, isn't he? Don't you think he's crazy?"

But "Crazy Henry" was able to sell his first Model T for $850 in 1908. By 1926, after streamlining production and quadrupling the average wage of his workers to $10 a day, he was selling the Model T to farmers and shop girls for $350.

A popular myth credits Henry Ford with inventing the "horseless carriage." Most people seem to think that he did. No! Henry Ford did not build the first car. He was the first to build the most cars in the least amount of time for the cheapest price. His dream of building "a motorcar for the multitudes" brought him a multitude of admirers.

Stand Up to Them!

**Those who say, "You'll never make a go of it!"
are not likely people who will ever "make a go of it."**

Whistling While You Practice

His best friend, Eduardo, told him that he had a "unique" voice. They often sang together during the summer at resorts around Naples, Italy. Eduardo convinced his friend to visit a prominent voice teacher to take lessons. But the plan backfired. The voice teacher was not impressed by the "unique" voice:

> **"My friend, your voice sounds like the whistling of the wind through a window."**

But those who packed the the Metropolitan Opera House in New York for his 607 appearances on that stage would beg to disagree. His was the "Voice of Gold" to opera buffs.

One of his early records, *Vesti la giubba*, sold more than a million copies. One of his performances was the subject of the first two radio broadcasts in history. For decades following his death, there was only one bust in the lobby of the Metropolitan—the bust of the great Italian tenor with the "unique" voice, Enrico Caruso.

Stand Up to Them!

Maybe all of the so-called experts are just whistling in the dark.

Let Your Fingers Do the Talking

At the conservatory, his first piano teacher told the 12 year old boy that he did not have the hands for mastering the keyboard. Nor did he have the technique or the aptitude for the piano.

His trombone teacher was just as adamant. "Now, my dear boy, listen to me. You are always trying to play *piano*. But why?" Without waiting for an answer, the trombone teacher muttered:

> **"Piano is useless for you—you have no future with the piano; your future is here, playing the trombone! . . . you will earn your living with the trombone, not with the piano."**

This young virtuoso was not tone deaf, but apparently he was deaf to criticism. After getting expelled from the conservatory twice, he persisted. He took private lessons from the best piano teacher in the conservatory. After four lessons, however, his private tutor was completely frustrated with this young protégé. His tickling of the ivories was not technically correct.

Refusing to give the boy any more lessons, he didn't hesitate to give him an earful:

> **"Now, I'll give you some good advice—do not try to play the piano, because you will never be a pianist. Never."**

That's funny! For more than 50 years, his name was a household word—synonymous with the piano. Other musicians hailed him "a pianist among pianists." He played to standing-room-only crowds who gave him rousing standing ovations. Queen Victoria hosted him at Windsor Castle and President Woodrow Wilson invited him to play in the White House.

In spite of the pitiful assessments of his teachers, Ignace Paderewski, the great Polish musician, became the twentieth century's first superstar. All over the world, wherever he performed, "Paddymania" broke out.

He worked at the piano. He didn't just play it. "His fingers glide over the keyboard," gushed one of his many fans, "as if it were all done by electricity."

But Paderewski did not just master the keyboard. He mastered his critics as well. Those who told him that he had no future with the piano did not understand his presence of mind.

Stand Up to Them!

**Those who think they know you best
have never seen you at your best . . . yet!**

Not Bullitt-Proof

The U.S. ambassador to France, a friend of the president, was someone whose views were highly-touted in the White House. He dared to offer this expert opinion:

**"There are no real leaders . . .
in all of England in this time
of grave crisis."**

Ambassador William Bullitt was right about one thing. It was a "time of grave crisis." On May 10, two million German troops, 136 divisions and their reserves, began their Blitzkrieg. Along a front 175 miles long, the Nazis smashed through the borders of France, Holland, Belgium, and Luxemborg. German paratroopers landed in Belgium, the Luftwaffe began bombing airfields in France and the Low Countries, and three Panzer divisions punched through the "impenetrable" Ardennes forest.

Five days later, Holland surrendered. Five days after Holland capitulated, the new prime minister of England received an urgent phone call from the French Premier. "We have been defeated!" shouted the Frenchman. "We are beaten! We have lost the battle." He was right. Within the month, Paris was occupied by the Nazis.

Late in the day on May 10, the same day that Hitler began his Blizkrieg—his "lightning strike"—the king of England accepted the resignation of Prime Minister Neville Chamberlain. With England in desperate need of a new prime minister, King George VI turned to an old "back–bencher" in the Parliament, a has-been, and demanded, "I want you to form a government."

This was the politician many had written off as "washed up" a decade earlier. He was a man who, by his own admission, had spent "eleven years in the political wilderness." But he was chosen prime minister in "this time of grave crisis" and his name is now synonymous with leadership.

With sheer grit and guts, Winston Churchill faced off against the Nazi menace as it was poised to strike across the English Channel. He warned the members of Parliament in his very first speech as prime minister:

> **"I have nothing to offer but blood, toil, tears, and sweat."**

Then he inspired them to believe they could defeat the Nazis:

> "You ask, what is our aim? I can answer in one word: It is victory, victory at all costs, victory in spite of all terror, victory however long and hard the road may be; for without victory, there is no survival."

A month after taking office, he received word that the French had surrendered. Churchill went on the air and vowed to the British people that they would continue the battle alone:

> "Hitler knows that he will have to break us on this island or lose the war. . . . Let us therefore brace ourselves to our duties, and so bear ourselves that if the British Empire and its commonwealth last for a thousand years, men will still say: This was their finest hour."

"No real leaders," indeed!

Stand Up to Them!

You might say, "I am not leadership material."
Who told you that, and why did you believe them?

Failing Forward

His first attempt to speak as a member of Parliament was a joke. Ben made a fool of himself that night. Another MP found his pitiful performance painful to watch:

> **"He made his first exhibition this night, beginning with florid assurance, speedily degenerating into ludicrous absurdity, and being at last put down with inextinguishable shouts of laughter."**

It was a miserable lecture, peppered with gobbledegook like "amatory eclogue" and "majestic mendicancy." His voice was drowned out by the hisses, hoots, laughter, and catcalls from his distinguished audience. But Ben displayed true grit with his parting shot. "Though I sit down now," he insisted, "the time will come when you will hear me."

In truth, his confidence was shot. He muttered to a loyal friend who tried to console him: "Failure!" His critics agreed. One moaned that Ben, "nearly killed the House." Another whined:

> **" . . . such a mixture of insolence and folly as I have never heard in my life before."**

This was not Ben's first and only failure. Prior to his 21st birthday, he forfeited a fortune that was not his to lose by dabbling in the stock market. His debts from those losses haunted him for years.

Assuming a role as the editor, of a newspaper, he was a miserable failure. His editorial debut was ridiculed as "tedious to a degree." Like that first speech in Parliament. Six months into his reign as its editor the paper was laid to rest in an early grave.

But Ben did not focus on his failures. As predicted, the time came when the other members of Parliament did "hear" him. Indeed, they did! Benjamin Disraeli, disparaged by many as a Jewish outcast, was elected Prime minister of England by the members of Parliament—TWICE!

Disraeli could boast that he was one of Queen Victoria's favorites. "Everyone likes flattery," he confided to a friend, "and when it comes to royalty, you should lay it on with a trowel." No wonder he was able to cement a durable relationship with England's longest reigning queen.

Stand Up to Them!

Have you ever been laughed at?
Remember: "He who laughs last, laughs best."

Can You Flunk
Sunday School?

One Sunday School teacher was sorely tempted to give one of his students an "F." Reviewing his evaluation of this young man, it would seem that a "D" would have been a show of mercy:

> **"I can truly say . . . that I have seen few persons whose minds were spiritually darker than was his when he came into my Sunday School class, and I think the committee of the Mt. Vernon Church seldom met an applicant for membership who seemed more unlikely ever to become a Christian of clear and decided views of gospel truth, still less to fill any sphere of public or extended usefulness."**

That Sunday School teacher and that church nearly flunked their most important test. They were tempted to overlook the tremendous potential in their most promising student and church member.

Dwight L. Moody was to the 19th century what Billy Graham was to the 20th century—the world's most influential evangelist in his generation. Picture this. Moody's home church almost said, "Thanks, but no thanks!"

Stand Up to Them!

**Others may not see much use for you,
but you can still be put to good use.**

A Presidential Forget-Me-Not

Newspapers trashed the President's speech the next day. *The Patriot and Union* of Harrisburg, PA, remembered it as forgettable:

> **"We pass over the silly remarks of the President; for the credit of the nation we are willing that the veil of oblivion shall be dropped over them and that they shall no more be repeated or thought of."**

The *Chicago Times* was equally brutal:

> **"The cheek of every American must tingle with shame as he reads the silly, flat, and dish-watery utterances of the man who has to be pointed out to intelligent foreigners as the President of the United States."**

The *Times* of London added insult to injury:

> **" . . . the ceremony was rendered ludicrous by some of the sallies of that poor President . . . Anything more dull and commonplace it would not be easy to produce."**

It was a brief speech delivered to a crowd estimated at fifteen thousand. These folks had already endured a lengthy, but eloquent speech delivered by the greatest orator of the day, Edward Everett. Mr. Everett's carefully prepared remarks were reprinted in many newspapers, occupying almost two full pages of newsprint. Everett's speech, "was the effort of his life," one enthusiast recalled. His poise and his oratorical skill held the attention of that huge audience for nearly two hours. Without the benefit of any type of public address system!

Everett's speech was peppered with flowery language:

> *"Overlooking these broad fields now reposing from the labors of the waning year . . ."*

> *"It is with hesitation that I raise my poor voice to break the eloquent silence of God and Nature."*

> *"I feel as never before, how truly it was said of old that it is sweet and becoming to die for one's country."*

> *"The whole earth is the sepulcher of illustrious men."*

His masterpiece was followed by a number performed by the Baltimore Glee Club. During their song, the President pulled his own "manuscript" from his coat pocket. He put on his glasses, glanced over the manuscript, and slid it back in his pocket. When the Glee Club finished, the President was introduced.

A reporter from the *Cincinnati Commercial* memorialized the moment with this biting critique:

> **The President rises slowly, draws from his pocket a paper, and, when commotion subsides, in a sharp, unmusical treble voice, reads the brief and pithy remarks.**

When the speech was concluded, the President confided to an old friend that his speech was a dud. "It is a flat failure and the people are disappointed," the President confessed.

Succeeding generations of Americans have passed their own judgment over these "silly remarks" that made the cheeks of old "tingle with shame." Most would not know the name of the noted orator, Edward Everett. They would have no clue that he spoke for two hours on this solemn occasion.

But scores of school-children have memorized "the brief and pithy remarks" uttered by the "sharp, unmusical treble voice" of the President. And most Americans, even today, would recognize that immortal introduction to the two-minute speech that Abraham Lincoln judged, "a flat failure."

You do remember how *The Gettysburg Address* begins, don't you?

"Fourscore and seven years ago . . . "

Stand Up to Them!

Determine to embarrass those who predict that you will prove to be an embarrassment.

Doubt Your Doubts

In his first big league game, he didn't get a hit in five trips to the plate. It was a discouraging start. His club finished the series against the Phillies and he still did not have a hit in 12 at-bats.

All the scouts who had watched him play in the minors said, "He can't miss!" But the 19-year-old rookie was scared spitless. He couldn't figure out why he was in the big leagues. Strolling into the manager's office before the start of the next game, he said:

"I ain't gonna make it. I can't hit up here. Why don't you just send me back?"

His manager knew that this kid had great potential. He didn't hesitate to assure the rookie, "No matter what you do, I'm sticking with you. . . . Now go out there and relax and play your game."

In the first inning of that game, the rookie got his first hit. He belted a home run over the left field roof off future hall-of-famer Warren Spahn. Then he failed to get a hit during the next three games. He was one for twenty-six.

But his manager was true to his word. He stuck with the kid, and it was a decision he would never live to regret. When the season ended, the youngster won Rookie of the Year honors.

During his career, he hit more than 50 home runs twice. When he finally hung up his spikes, he had a total of 660 home runs, earning him third place behind Hank Aaron and Babe Ruth. But he wasn't just a slugger. This kid succeeded in hitting over .300 in ten different seasons and finished with a stellar .302 lifetime batting average.

He wasn't just a great hitter, either. He had blazing speed, a strong throwing arm, and a gold glove. Hall of Fame baseball announcer,

Ernie Harwell, argued that his "fielding was even more spectacular than his hitting. Great speed and a strong arm enabled him to make catches I have never seen by any other player."

In a game against the Pirates, he raced across the outfield to snare a line drive with his bare hand. "It was the greatest catch I have ever seen," Harwell claimed. For the rest of us mortals, the unforgettable catch was one he made with his back to home plate racing toward the centerfield wall, robbing a batter of an easy double or triple.

People often ask Ernie Harwell, "Who's the greatest player you've ever seen?" There is no doubt in his mind: "Willie Mays." Willie had his doubts in his rookie season. But no one else ever did.

Stand Up to Them!

**What if, "I can't do it!" equals
"I haven't done it yet!"?**

A Snicker-Tape Parade

People denounced him as a, "hypocrite," an "impostor," and . . .

"little better than a murderer."

Crowds jeered him and hissed at him as he rode through the streets. A newspaper cartoon conjured up the perfect ending for this fiend. It depicted him facing a guillotine, the razor-sharp blade poised to sever his head.

Who was this vile scoundrel? None other than the celebrated hero of the Revolutionary War and the first President of the United States. Yes, George Washington.

In his day he got no respect. Today we revere him as "the Father of our Country."

Stand Up to Them!

**Anyone can be a critic, but not everyone
can stand up to criticism. Can you?**

Right Idea, Wrong Tome

As a medical doctor, it was perfectly natural for Peter to presume that his greatest legacy would be his scientific studies and experiments. He presented a paper to the Royal Society of London with the cryptic title, "Explanation of an Optical Deception in the Appearance of the Spokes of a Wheel Seen Through Vertical Apertures."

As strange as that convoluted description sounds today, his paper had an important influence on at least one useful invention. But Peter received no credit for his contribution to the motion picture industry.

> **He was sure that a two-volume work published in 1834 would perpetuate his name and reputation for centuries. It was his *Animal and Vegetable Physiology Considered with Reference to Natural Theology.***

Good luck trying to find it! You've probably never heard of it. But, you have heard of Peter. Especially if you like to write. Or work crossword puzzles. He was on-the-mark when he assumed that he would be remembered for one of his books. But he was wrong about which one.

Contrary to what Peter thought, he is not remembered as a scientist. It is not for his accomplishments in his professional life that he is remembered. He is famous for his hobby.

Peter had an insatiable love for words and how they are used. In his late twenties, he bought a notebook and began compiling and classifying lists of English words. He would have agreed with Mark Twain. "The difference between the right word, and the almost right word," Twain argued, "is the difference between lightning and the lightning bug."

When he was 73 years old, Dr. Peter Mark Roget published his classifications of words as the *Thesaurus of English Words and Phrases*. Roget's *Thesaurus* has sold zillions of copies. However, "If Roget knew that millions of people would use his book to do crossword puzzles," someone quipped, "he would probably be deeply offended."

Maybe. But he would be pleased to know that he has not been forgotten.

Stand Up to Them!

Don't forget! You will be remembered for something. Make it something worth remembering.

Turned Down,
But Not Out

Unemployed during the Depression, Charles B. Darrow had too much time on his hands. He snatched up a piece of oilcloth, some scraps of cardboard, a few knick-knacks, and got creative. Voila! His new product was ready to be tested. It was an instant success with his friends.

Darrow started selling his creation, but couldn't handle the flood of new orders. He contacted a company that specialized in the type of product that he had designed.

**The company turned it down, complaining that
the product had 52 fundamental errors in it.**

Corporate heads argued that it took too long to achieve the anticipated results. (Something many people have found frustrating over the years.) The instructions were too difficult to follow, company execs groused. And the ultimate goal was not clear, they grumbled, especially for children.

In 1935, the same company had second thoughts. They went out on a limb and bought the product from Darrow. In less than two months, orders for 20,000 sets were flooding the company every week! Since then, millions upon millions of table-top sets have been sold.

Software versions of the product are available on CD-ROM today. Internet users meet in cyber-space to challenge one another to play Darrow's game. Conservative estimates suggest that more than 250 million people world-wide have enjoyed and been entertained by it.

But what about poor Charles Darrow? He went from being nearly destitute during the early days of the Depression to one of a select few millionaires created during the 1930s.

The game that Darrow created from a piece of oilcloth and scraps of cardboard is a classic. His oilcloth square was transformed into a game board. His knick-knacks have been adopted as the playing pieces. Simple scraps of cardboard became colorful deeds to various properties. These were named after actual places in Atlantic City, where Charles often vacationed.

Charles Darrow's complex and complicated game, *Monopoly*, is now one of the most popular board games in the world. It made Parker Brothers famous, even though the company initially rejected it.

Stand Up to Them!

Those who can only find "fundamental errors" might be guilty of making a fundamental error.

"Horse and Buggy" Limits

It was a serious letter that seems silly by today's standards. A concerned citizen wrote to the president of the United States:

"The Almighty certainly never intended that people should travel at such breakneck speed."

A new "evil" was about to be foisted upon an unsuspecting populace, this nay-sayer suggested. He warned that it would kill business, boost unemployment, and weaken the national defense. Try not to giggle when you read this letter:

The canal system of this country is being threatened by the spread of a new form of transportation known as "railroads." The federal government must preserve the canals for the following reasons:

One. If canal boats are supplanted by 'railroads,' serious unemployment will result. Captains, cooks, drivers, hostlers, repairmen and lock tenders will be left without means of livelihood, not to mention the numerous farmers now employed in growing hay for horses.

Two. Boat builders would suffer, and towline, whip and harness makers would be left destitute.

Three. Canal boats are absolutely essential to the defense of the United States. In the event of the expected trouble with England, the Erie Canal would be the only means by which we could ever move the supplies so vital to waging modern war.

As you may well know, Mr. President, "railroad" carriages are pulled at the enormous speed of 15 miles per hour by "engines" which, in addition to endangering life and limb of passengers, roar and snort their way through the countryside, setting fire to crops, scaring the livestock and frightening women

and children. The Almighty certainly never intended
that people should travel at such breakneck speed.

Can you imagine? Fifteen miles an hour was touted as "breakneck speed." Hold on for dear life! In our "space age" of supersonic transports and Space Shuttles, it is hard to comprehend these "horse and buggy" limits.

However, the unemployment concerns were real. Canal boat captains and lock tenders were put out to pasture. But the railroad industry employed more than its fair share of the work force in the 19th century. And who can hope to remember a day when canal boats were considered vital to the national defense!

Change is never easy, but it was harder than ever when changes were few. Mark Twain unveiled the spirit of his age with regard to change when he wrote, "The only person who likes change is a wet baby."

This letter reflects our ever-present resistance to change. You know—that "We've never done it that way before" mentality. Funny thing is, the letter was written on January 31, 1829, and addressed to President Andrew Jackson.

The author of this desperate appeal was Martin Van Buren. At the time, he was the governor of New York. But he was destined to succeed Andrew Jackson as President of the United States. Imagine that!

Stand Up to Them!

**Change is never easy,
but it is an unchangeable fact of life.**

Permission to Fail,
Not to Quit

On December 23, 1988, the United Technologies Corporation published this little ditty in *The Wall Street Journal*:

> You've failed many times, although you don't
> remember.
> You fell down the first time you tried to walk.
> You almost drowned the first time you tried to
> swim.
> Did you hit the ball the first time you swung a bat?

This perky item included a reminder about a businessman whose track record was poor. Literally! Rowland had opened and closed four stores between 1843 and 1855. He had to declare bankruptcy on all four occasions. He wrote in his ledger during those years:

"I have worked for two years for nothing."

Actually, he worked twelve years for nothing. Or was it? During those years marked with dismal failures he developed certain theories about what his customers wanted and how to meet their expectations.

In 1858 this perennial failure opened another "fancy" dry goods store with only an 11-foot store front on Sixth Avenue in Manhattan. Rowland's sales the first day were a meager $11.06. "Could this be my fifth store to go under?" he must have wondered.

But he persevered and over the next 20 years acquired the leases on 11 neighboring buildings. He expanded his store as both sales and inventory grew.

Rowland undersold his competitors with rock-bottom prices and advertised aggressively. Store ads barked at customers, "Our goods shall be sold cheap! Our goods shall be sold cheap!" Not great ad copy by Madison Avenue standards. But it worked.

Year after year he added to the variety and number of goods that he sold. His store looked like a patchwork-quilt of departments offering clothes, jewelry, toiletries, kitchen utensils, plants, toys, and dolls displayed in a labyrinth of connecting rooms in adjacent buildings.

In 1861, Rowland started a mail-order business. Two years later, he pioneered the use of annual clearance sales—now a staple in department stores. Shoppers from Brooklyn and cities like Hoboken and Jersey City across the Hudson River were offered free delivery.

Seasonal displays of dolls and mechanical toys in store windows were another of Rowland's innovations. In 1870, he added a soda fountain.

By 1875, the store's motto, "We will not be undersold," was immortalized. It was the world's first, full-fledged department store by the time of Rowland's death in 1877. However, the term "department store" did not come into vogue until the 1890s.

The famous five-pointed red-star trademark was developed from a tattoo sported by the store's founder. It was a memento from the days when Rowland had hunted whales in the Pacific.

In 1902, 25 years after Rowland's death, the store was moved 20 blocks north to Herald Square in Manhattan. This 2.1 million-square-foot flagship store occupies an entire city block and, for half a century, was the largest store in the country.

Life magazine celebrated the store's size and success in December 1948, when it declared, "It is not merely the physically biggest store in the world, selling the greatest variety of items (400,000), it is also the world's largest drugstore, bookstore, furniture store and fabric and china store."

Remember the poem from *The Wall Street Journal*? Here is how it ends:

> Heavy hitters, the ones who hit the most home runs,
>   also strike out a lot. . . .
> Babe Ruth struck out 1,330 times but he also hit
>   714 home runs.
> Don't worry about failure.
> Worry about the chances you miss when you don't
>   even try.

Apparently, Rowland Hussey Macy, the founder of Macy's Department Store, did not worry about striking out a lot. He knew that failure is never final and seldom fatal. In the twentieth century, his store—his eighth attempt at retail sales—was one of the most famous retail establishments in the world.

Even for those who have never shopped there, Macy's holds a special place in their hearts. They know the store because of its prominent role in the annual Thanksgiving Day Parade. Or because it was immortalized in one of the more popular Christmas movies, *The Miracle on 34th Street*. Yes, Broadway and 34th Street, that is the address for R.H. Macy's success *store-y* in the twentieth century.

Stand Up to Them!

**Everyone who is successful has had failures.
Successful people make their failures work for them.**

Not a "Sound" Decision!

Not long after the birth of "rock 'n' roll," a record company offered this lame explanation for refusing a contract to a small band:

**"We don't like their sound.
Groups of guitars are on their way out."**

When the band's agent tried to appeal the decision, the executives from the record company dug in their heels. This group "won't go," they sniffed. "We know these things. You have a record business . . . why not stick to that?"

But this group's agent knew how to handle rejection. He went to two other record companies and braved the same response: "No thanks!"

One other record company, EMI, had expressed similar sentiments before the other three. "Whilst we appreciate the talents of this group," wrote the general marketing manager, "we feel that we have sufficient groups of this type at the present time under contract and that it would not be advisable for us to sign any further contract of this nature at present."

Six months later, an executive with EMI's weakest record label signed the group to a contract. An embarrassed general marketing manager felt compelled to explain, "Even Artistes Managers are human and can change their minds!"

It was a real gamble for EMI's *Parlophone* label. They specialized in comedy records. A rock 'n' roll group was a stretch. Especially a group inspired by singing sensations from the U.S. —performers like Chuck Berry, Elvis Presley, and Bill Haley. Their music was a throw-back to the early energy of rock and roll.

In those days folk songs by groups like the *Kingston Trio* and *Peter, Paul, and Mary* were the rage. Coffee houses multiplied like rabbits around many college campuses to stage this new "pop" music.

Rock 'n' roll had to take a back seat. People wondered, "Whatever happened to that good ol' rock 'n' roll?" How could anyone blame the Decca Recording Company for saying "No!" to a guitar band?

"But the times," as Bob Dylan crooned, "they [were] a changin'." Rock bands were electrifying audiences by the mid-1960s. "Groups of guitars" weren't "on their way out." Teens countered that they were "Way out, man!"

Rock groups, "jamming" with their guitars, sold millions and millions of records in the 1960's. Their names are the stuff of legends: the *Rolling Stones, The Byrds, Cream, The Grateful Dead, Jefferson Airplane, The Doors,* and the *Allman Brothers Band.*

So Decca was wrong! "Groups of guitars" weren't on their way out in 1962. Neither was the group that Decca turned down. At one point this band had *eight* songs in the Top Ten! That was in 1964, two years after Decca said, "No!"

The band's members are not just famous rock stars. They are legends in the music industry!

At a recent auction of the band's memorabilia, 300 items were sold for $1.46 million. A violin bass guitar sold for $202,955. Another guitar signed by one of the band members went for $121,773. Even a guitar strap fetched $16,236. Isn't that incredible?

When Decca Recording Company said "No!" to the "Fab Four" they had no way of knowing how wrong they were. That confounded group of guitars—the instruments themselves— would be worth half a million dollars one day.

Chalk it up to "Beatlemania." The B-E-A-T-L-E-S (John, Paul, George, and Ringo) and their agent, Brian Epstein, did not take kindly to the word "No!"

Stand Up to Them!

Those who don't like the way you sound may not be thinking very sound.

A Declaration of Indignation

The president of a major university warned that if a particular candidate was elected to the nation's highest office . . .

"We may see our wives and daughters the victims of prostitution, soberly dishonored, speciously polluted; the outcasts of delicacy and virtue, the loathing of God and man."

You might not be as surprised, if you were to discover that this was a denunciation of Adolf Hitler or Benito Mussolini. But it wasn't!

Yale University President, Timothy Dwight, made this alarming prediction concerning Thomas Jefferson. Yes, the same Thomas Jefferson who wrote *The Declaration of Independence*!

Stand Up to Them!

It doesn't matter what they say about you as long as you don't let it be true of you.

"I Can't!" Won't Do!

A young man went to hear his friend preach his first sermon. He walked away with a favorable impression of his friend, but with grave doubts about himself:

> **"I'd give anything in the world if I could stand up in front of people like Grady did and preach. That'll never happen to me, I know."**

It wasn't that he didn't try. Sometimes he joined some of his friends when they were preaching from a soapbox. But he was rather timid and fumbled his way through his messages.

However, the average person on the street today has never heard of this young man's friend. Do you recognize the name Grady Wilson? Probably not.

But you will recognize the name of the young man who had serious doubts about his own preaching ability. Billy Graham has preached to more people than anyone else in the history of the world . . . besides appearing on the list of the most admired men in America every year.

Stand Up to Them!

You can still make it happen even when you don't think you can.

They Really "Missed the Boat"

A rich man can be a poor fool. John Jacob Astor, one of the elites of New York "high society," proved that when he muttered with great disdain:

"We are safer here than in that little boat."

He could not have made a more tragic mistake. Two hours later the *Titanic* sank into the icy waters of the North Atlantic.

This great ship was reputed to be unsinkable. Everyone said so. Maybe that is why there were only enough lifeboats to rescue 1,100 people. 2,200 passengers and crew were aboard the ship on its maiden voyage.

Captain Edward J. Smith, who was 59 years old, planned to retire after this trip across the North Atlantic. Smith took command of every new ship in the *White Star Line* when it set sail on its maiden voyage. Six years earlier, as captain of the *Adriatic*, he had boasted:

"I cannot imagine any condition which would cause a ship to founder. I cannot conceive of any vital disaster happening to this vessel. Modern shipbuilding has gone beyond that."

Now he stood on the bridge of a ship twice the size of the *Adriatic*—and, presumably, twice as safe. However, the ship's builder had just informed him that, with the damage the *Titanic* had sustained, it wouldn't float for long.

Nobody expected this ship to sink. In Southhampton, prior to departure, Mrs. Albert Caldwell, one of the passengers on the fateful voyage, asked a deck hand, "Is this ship really unsinkable?" He sniffed:

**"Yes, lady. God himself
could not sink this ship."**

After the *Titanic* collided with the iceberg, most people on board shrugged off the danger. One passenger asked someone standing nearby, "What do they say is the trouble?" His fellow passenger replied, "Icebergs."

"Well, I guess it's nothing serious," predicted the first passenger, "I'm going back to my cabin to read."

It would not be a good read.

Someone woke a member of the crew from a dead sleep. He held in his hand a chunk of ice the size of a teacup. "There are tons of ice forward!" he cried. "Oh, well," the sleepy steward yawned, "that will not hurt." Then he rolled over to go back to sleep. But sleep would be the last thing on his mind, shortly.

The ship that could not sink soon could no longer float. When the *Titanic* disappeared beneath the waves on April 15, 1912, it took 1,513 people to a watery grave on the ocean bottom.

Stand Up to Them!

**Confidence is a good thing,
if it is not placed in the wrong thing.**

One "Yes" Trumps
Twenty "No's"

Chester Carlson succeeded! He created a machine to do what he had dreamed of a machine doing for years. But when he went out to find a corporate sponsor to help bring it to the market, no one shared his enthusiasm.

More than twenty companies, including RCA, General Electric, and IBM rejected his machine.

It was a primitive version of a machine you have used over and over again. But this one was encased in a wooden box. "It was just hard to put over because the materials were so crude," Chester admitted. "It wasn't likely to excite a businessman."

His workshop was primitive, too. He couldn't afford a lab. The kitchen in his apartment in Queens served as his laboratory. Later, he moved his workshop to a small room in the back of a beauty shop owned by his mother-in-law. It was a makeshift lab and he had to work with the rawest of raw materials.

"I did give up a few times," Chester confessed, "and I tried to forget it. But I was so convinced it was important, I couldn't let it rest."

He was nearly broke and at his wit's end when there was a significant breakthrough. The Battelle Memorial Institute in Columbus, Ohio, agreed to help research and develop Chester's invention. Battelle (a non-profit research group) discovered the project was too expensive for their budget, however. They began looking for a corporate sponsor to underwrite their research and development on Chester's machine.

Every major corporation that Battelle contacted expressed zero interest in this new invention. It was the Haloid Company, a small manufacturer of photographic supplies in Rochester, New York, that ultimately took interest in Chester's invention.

Battelle and Haloid unveiled the machine and the process that they had developed on a special anniversary. It was ten years to the day after Chester's first successful demonstration of his invention. Their presentation was made to a meeting of the Optical Society of America. It was greeted with a yawn. The technology was intriguing, but no one *saw* a use for it.

One year later, Haloid marketed their first machine. It was crude and primitive in design, and was nicknamed the "ox box." Haloid executives were stunned that it was so poorly received in the market-place. But they didn't give up.

Six years later, they introduced a new model that had modest success in the market. Five more years passed before the company introduced a version of Chester's machine that found broad market appeal. After investing sixty million dollars in the project, their new model was the size of a freezer and weighed six hundred pounds. But it could be operated with the push of a button.

Haloid decided not to sell the machines but to lease them. For $95 a month, a company could lease the machine and acquire a service contract with Haloid. The company's revenues skyrocketed.

From total sales of $32 million in 1959, they vaulted to $60 million in sales in 1961. Revenues nearly doubled in two years. After that the growth of the company was exponential. Total sales in 1966 roared past the $500 million mark.

Chester, who was never hired by Haloid, retired a wealthy man. He received royalties for his invention based on his agreement with Battelle. By the mid-1960s, his wealth was estimated at $150 million. He spent the rest of his life giving away $100 million to various research projects and charities.

By now, you are probably itching to know what Chester's machine was designed to do. He described the process as *electrophotography*. "I recognized a very great need," he recalled "for a machine that could be right in an office where you could bring a document to it, push it in a slot and get a copy out."

A Greek scholar helped give a name to the process that Haloid thought was "user-friendly" in the market. He recommended that they call it *xerography* (from *xeros* for "dry" and *graphos* for "writing"). Since the machine used a dry chemical process for duplicating documents, the name fit.

Haloid changed its name twice while bringing their copier to the market. Since they called their earliest version a XeroX (hence the nickname "ox box"), they changed the name of the company to Haloid Xerox in 1958. But in 1961, they streamlined their identity for the marketplace. Haloid became known as Xerox.

Think of it! IBM, GE, RCA, and roughly twenty other companies said "No!" to Chester Carlson's primitive *electrophotography* machine. And the Optical Society of America had too little vision to see the value of the technological innovations of *xerography*.

Today you might have a Sharp or Canon copier in your office. But, how many times have you asked an assistant, "Could you *xerox* a copy of this for me?" Can you imagine asking, "Could you IBM this, or GE this for me?" It doesn't have the same ring to it, does it?

Stand Up to Them!

**No matter how many people say, "No!"
keep looking for the one who will say, "Yes!"**

When The Hunter
Becomes The Hunted

King Louis XVI of France preferred hunting to ruling. He considered any day that he failed to shoot a stag a waste. During one fifteen-year period, he bagged 1,274 of them. One afternoon, after returning from a day's hunt empty-handed, he wrote in his diary:

"July 14: Nothing."

It was a tragic understatement! One of history's great little ironies. July 14, 1789 would be something, indeed!

That day eight thousand Paris citizens stormed the Bastille and sparked the French Revolution. Louis XVI was greeted when he returned to Versailles by news of the revolt. Six months later, he was beheaded like a common criminal on a guillotine, the ghastly symbol of the revolution that had claimed his throne and now his life.

July 14 is *not* "Nothing!" to the French today. They celebrate it as "Bastille Day," their Independence Day.

Stand Up to Them!

**When nothing seems to be happening,
watch for something major to happen!**

Not Just A Housewife

Have you ever wondered what famous people were like before they paraded onto the world's stage? "Did friends describe her as 'Miss Personality' in her high school yearbook?" Or, "Was he voted 'Most likely to succeed' by his peers?" you might wonder.

Consider this case study of a young lady who grew up to become famous. In a comparison with her own sister, she recalled,

> **"Lee was the pretty one. So I guess I was supposed to be the intelligent one."**

A relative, likewise, remembered her as being quite ordinary: "At age fifteen my cousin was prissy, bookish and bossy." Her cousin's reflections were not flattering, to say the least.

She seemed to be money-hungry, ". . . primarily because she didn't have any."

> **"She was too much, 'de trop' in French—a perfectly horrible child. . . . She was a master manipulator."**

Despite the accusation of being money-hungry, this young lady was not overly ambitious. In fact, in her high school yearbook, she wrote next to the entry, "ambition in life"—"Not to be a housewife."

Her fiance's family thought she was flighty. His sisters tagged her, "The Debutante." They ridiculed her voice, nicknaming her "Babykins." She told her future sisters-in-law that she hoped to become a ballet dancer someday. One objected, "With those feet of yours! You'd be better off going into soccer, kid."

Those put-downs seem comical in retrospect. Years later, one of her brother-in-laws paid tribute to her distinctive achievements with these words: "No one else looked like her, spoke like her, wrote like her or was so original in the way she did things."

This was a woman who fascinated people everywhere with her majestic manners and feminine mystique. She was a model of both fashion and style. Admirers remember this amazing woman as chic, elegant, and beautiful. She waltzed onto the world's stage with grace and dignity, and exited from this life as one of the most respected and beloved women of modern times.

One of her neighbors, who knew this young lady as a socially awkward teenager, remembered her as someone who was intellectually sharp and someone who was going places. There was only one address this neighbor never could picture in her friend's future—1600 Pennsylvania Avenue.

"The only future I would never have predicted for her is First Lady. She didn't have the personality that goes with the job."

Isn't that funny? She was describing the First Lady who was credited with turning the White House into "a showcase for American art and history." Many Americans remember her as the closest thing to royalty that we've ever had. The "Queen of Camelot."

No matter how much John Kennedy's image may fade in the future, Jackie Kennedy Onassis will be remembered as, "the best and the brightest."

Stand Up to Them!

Don't expect less of yourself just because "they" don't expect much of you.

An E-Ticket Ride

Best-sellers these days are peppered with sex. His book had none. And, it was too technical. Nobody expected the book to sell a bunch of copies. Least of all him.

"I thought we'd sell maybe 5,000 or 10,000 hardcovers and that would be the end of it. I never really thought about making money."

His dream since high school had been to see his name splashed on the cover of a book. When he majored in English at Baltimore's Loyola College, he dreamed of writing a novel. Years later, as an insurance broker in his mid-thirties, he hit bottom. His agency serviced more than 1,100 clients. "But the insurance business," he realized, "was not intellectually satisfying."

Insurance did afford him one luxury, however. He was his own boss. He made the rules, and he could decide to take time to make his dream come true. In three months time, he completed the first draft of a 400-page novel.

He discovered that he didn't enjoy the grind of putting his thoughts on paper. "Writing is miserably difficult work," he admitted. For him, research is the "fun part."

Sensing the novel was ready for public consumption, he started to hunt for a publisher. But not for one of the "big boys" in New York. He didn't rate their attention as far as he was concerned. His previous qualifications were a letter to the editor and a brief article on the MX missile that he had submitted for publication.

Judging that no one else would take him seriously, he drove up the road to Annapolis, MD. Maybe, he surmised, the Naval Institute Press would appreciate his work. They responded in three weeks. They did like it. But they wanted him to rewrite the entire novel.

Some writers-to-be might have tossed in their pens at that point. He didn't. Eighteen months later he relished in the fruit of his labors—his book displayed on store shelves. But without any fanfare.

Surprise! Nobody expected the enthusiastic response the book received. Ronald Reagan, at the height of his popularity as President, endorsed the story as "the perfect yarn." That catapulted the novel onto *The New York Times* bestseller list. It enjoyed a seven month reign on top. Enthusiastic readers hyped it as an "E-ticket ride."

Rear admirals in the U.S. Navy and intelligence experts marveled that an insurance broker knew so many "classified secrets." Officials at the Pentagon debriefed him. They were eager to find out how he obtained detailed knowledge about certain weapon systems.

Nobody could pinpoint a genre for a novel like this. It didn't fit any traditional ones, which led to the creation of the term "Techno-Thriller." Jack Higgins, a master of thrillers, warned his peers that this might be just the first of many. "The rest of us better look out," Higgins teased, "because God alone knows what the second and third are going to be like."

Little did he know.

To date a dozen of the Techno-Thriller's novels have been "mega-bestsellers." Half of those have produced blockbuster movies featuring Hollywood's A-list.

As an aspiring author who did not think that his book would sell more than five or ten thousand copies, he has surprised many. None more than he himself.

USA Today reported that his first four novels sold 30 million copies. His fourth novel earned him a $4 million advance. Reporters still try to calculate the dollar signs of his most recent advance. "It was . . . large," he admits with a coy smile.

What a remarkable run for an insurance broker who had never set foot on a submarine! *The Hunt for Red October*, the story of a cat-and-mouse chase after a renegade Russian nuclear submarine, did not suffer as a result of Tom Clancy's lack of personal experience.

Stand Up to Them!

**You don't have to see the "big picture",
just picture yourself doing your best.**

A Duell Mistake

It was a strange statement for someone like Charles Duell to make. It meant death to his profession. He urged President William McKinley to abolish his federal agency. All because he was convinced that,

> **"Everything that can be invented
> has been invented."**

Since Duell's day, we have abandoned the steam engine in favor of atomic fusion. We have graduated from pen and paper to a keyboard and mouse. A ton of gadgets were waiting to be invented.

Part of Charles Duell's error was the timing of his remark. He forecast the death of inventions in 1899, on the eve of the 20th century. More than 4 million patents have been filed since then.

What makes Duell's prediction most ironic is the identity of his job-title. At the time, Duell was the commissioner of the United States Patent and Trademark Office.

Stand Up to Them!

**Don't stop plowing ahead into the future
just because others are stuck in the past.**

A Population Implosion?

He wasn't the kind of guy whose head was buried in the sand. Maybe in a pile of books, but definitely not in sand. He was a philosopher, a thinking "man's man." But don't go thinking that his high I.Q. qualifies this as a *smart* remark:

> **"The population of the earth decreases every day, and, if this continues, in another ten centuries the earth will be nothing but a desert."**

Not a population explosion. A population *implosion*! This sage argued that the human race was in danger of undercutting itself, not overpopulating the earth. Where was Paul Ehrlich's *Population Bomb* when we needed it?

Yet, some of our contemporary population gurus would agree with our philosophical friend on one salient point. They would agree that the earth could wind up a desert—because of the stresses introduced by a mushrooming population. . . not because the last man standing couldn't find a woman to mother his children.

Consider some important points to contrast with this wise guy's prediction:

- More people live in China today than were alive when this sage made his prediction.
- A professor from the University of Minnesota insists that three-fifths of all the people ever born are alive today.
- It wasn't until 1853 that the human race reached the one billion population milestone. Since that time, note the exponential growth:

1853 to 1930	2 billion	(77 yrs)
1930 to 1961	3 billion	(31 yrs)
1961 to 1976	4 billion	(15 yrs)
1976 to 1986	5 billion	(10 yrs)
1986 to 2001	6 billion	(15 yrs)

Does that look like a downward spiral to you?

Did you guess that it must have been one of those ancient Greek philosophers who made this stupid prediction about earth's dramatic population decrease? Not so! The culprit was a French sage by the name of Montesquieu. Believe it or not, he made his dire prediction in 1743 A.D., not 1743 B.C.

He saw the "future," and we weren't in it. At least not for long. But that's O.K. Most of us weren't aware of his existence . . . until now!

Stand Up to Them!

Make sure that those who predict trends aren't reading their charts upside down.

Bigotry Is Not
Big of You

It was the presidential version of "Guess Who's Coming for Dinner?" A reporter for the *Washington Post* saw the guest list from the White House. One name rang a bell and led him to write an item for the morning edition of the *Post*. He mentioned this gentleman, by name, as a guest who had "dined with the President last evening."

Despite the obscure location of the piece, it got noticed. Not by Washington insiders, but by the correspondents of several newspapers in the South. One paper, the *Memphis Scimitar*, charged that the President had committed:

> **"the most damnable outrage ever perpetrated by any citizen of the United States when he invited a n_____ to dine with him at the White House."**

Other editors followed suit, venom dripping from their pens! The *New Orleans Times-Democrat* shrieked, "White men of the South, how do you like it? White women of the South, how do YOU like it?"

The *Raleigh Post* vented in a rhyme:

> "Precedents are cast aside—put aside with vigor;
> Black and white sit side by side, as Roosevelt dines a
> n_____."

One cartoon had a racist caricature of the President with a black face, wearing his signature spectacles and showing his pearly whites in a goofy grin. Another lampooned his "Negro Policy," depicting the President on a park bench hugging a black man in a monkey suit.

Republican Teddy Roosevelt, the famed "Rough Rider," faced a tough tour of duty in the Oval Office. Especially in the South, which voted almost exclusively for Democrats. This editorial lynching occurred just five weeks after Roosevelt moved into the White House in 1901.

T. R. counseled others to "Speak softly, but carry a big stick." But he refused to strike back. Expressing his own regret about the episode, Roosevelt explained, "The very fact that I felt a moment's qualm on inviting him because of his color, made me ashamed of myself and made me hasten to send the invitation."

Would you like to know whose "coming to dinner" caused such a commotion? He was the man who, " . . . best embodied the standard of personal character and civic virtue for other Negroes to imitate," Roosevelt maintained.

You might recognize the name of Roosevelt's guest, but you may not know why. Read on, and you will find out why you do, or why you should recognize him.

This distinguished White House guest was born a slave in the deep South. He was set free and, as a boy, went to work in a salt furnace and a coal mine. To get an education, he attended night school until he graduated at 16. To further his education, he hiked 500 miles to the Hampton Normal and Agricultural Institute in Virginia. Working as a janitor, he was able to pay his school bill. He graduated a schoolteacher.

With several years of experience under his belt, he was invited to head up the Tuskegee Institute in rural Alabama. It was housed in a small shanty and an old, decrepit church building. Eking out a meager existence, the Institute boasted a budget of just $2,000 a year when its new director arrived.

Thirty-four years later, when he died, the Institute had 100 well-equipped buildings, 1,500 students, a faculty approaching 200, and an endowment of $2 million. Under his leadership, it acquired a reputation as the premier institute for vocational training for black men and women in the United States.

This "premier black leader," Booker T. Washington, was Teddy Roosevelt's controversial dinner guest in 1901. Their meeting served as a signpost for others in the 20th century, pointing to the desperate need for further integration of the races. By their quiet and dignified examples, both men made bigots appear to be what they actually are . . . small-minded.

Stand Up to Them!

**Expressions of outrage can
turn out to be outrageous!**

A Dollar For Your Thoughts

You don't need to twist the arm of John or Jane Doe American to get them to affirm that a U.S. Senator can make mistakes. It is increasingly more difficult to convince voters that senators are capable of anything else. So maybe it won't surprise you to discover that a senator dared to go public with this huge blunder:

> **"I have never heard of anything, and I cannot conceive of anything more ridiculous, more absurd, and more affrontive to all sober judgment than the cry that we are profiting by the acquisition . . . I hold that they are not worth a dollar!"**

But it might surprise you to discover which distinguished senator said this about what incredible bargain. The senator was one of America's truly great statesmen, Daniel Webster. The year was 1848. The purchase in question was for two new territories in the west: New Mexico and California.

Wouldn't you be willing to sacrifice a buck for one or the other?

Stand Up to Them!

**Opinions like, "You aren't worth much!"
aren't really worth a whole lot.**

A Fly-by-Night Prediction

There have been critics of manned flight as long as there have been those who have dared to dream about it. "If God had meant man to fly . . . ." Well, you know that drill!

But one man who poured cold water on those not-so-idle dreamers should have known better when he argued:

> "The demonstration that no possible combination of known substances, known forms of machinery, and known forms of force can be united in a practical machine by which man shall fly long distances through the air, seems to the writer as complete as it is possible for the demonstration of any physical fact to be."

Or, in plain English:

"Flight by machines heavier than air is unpractical and insignificant . . . utterly impossible."

This genius, who was wide of the mark on that call, was a scientist who made many significant contributions in his field. He wrote a series of papers that were "remarkable" for their "sustained high quality." According to one scholar, "Hardly anything in them has proved to be incorrect, and at mid-twentieth century they were still worthy of the attention of any student . . . ."

What you may find quite interesting is that this prize-winning scientist, Simon Newcomb, was an astronomer and a mathematician. One of his remarkable achievements was an elaborate set of calculations of the orbits and rotations of the planets and moons in our solar system.

Wouldn't he be surprised to discover that not only has man flown, but that there has been a man on the moon? A real man in real space—in real time. More than once!

Would you like to know when Simon Newcomb made his ill-timed prediction that man was not capable of designing a flying machine?

He made his pronouncement in October 1903, two months before the Wright Brothers achieved the first powered flight (12 seconds long) in Kitty Hawk, North Carolina, on December 17th.

Stand Up to Them!

**Something is only "utterly impossible"
until someone actually does it!**

What A Flop!

Did you ever try the high jump? Maybe in gym class. At least once? It really *is* as difficult as it looks, isn't it?

During the Olympic Games in 1900, an athlete by the name of Irving Baxter high jumped 6'2". That didn't leave much room for improvement, according to the experts.

They said the invisible barrier was 7 feet.
No one would ever clear a bar at 7 feet.

High Jump techniques vary. Only one convention is required of the athletes: they must take off from one foot. The old-fashioned technique was the scissors kick. Athletes cleared the bar in an upright position with a distinctive kick. It was succeeded by the popular Western roll and straddle. Rather than upright, the athlete's body was parallel to the bar in a horizontal position.

In the 1960s, one notorious rebel concluded that the other high jumpers were approaching the bar and the seven-foot barrier all wrong. He would race toward the bar, dive backward, and twist his body over the bar. People ridiculed this young upstart for his unorthodox style.

Critics dubbed this bizarre technique, "the Fosbury flop." But in 1968, when Richard Fosbury "flopped" over the seven-foot mark head first (and backwards), he had the last laugh. More recently an East German cleared 7'8³/₄".

Wasn't seven feet supposed to be the upper limit?

Maybe you can boast that you tried the high jump. But what about pole vaulting? Did you ever have the guts to try that fool's errand? Athletes race 30 to 45 meters, thrust their pole into that tiny slot called the slideway, and then spring high into the air. Hopefully, they vault forward, clear the bar and drop safely into the padded pit.

In theory, that's how it's supposed to work. But most of us have had visions of falling the wrong way, which caused us to make the right decision. Never to try it!

In 1956, 15 feet was considered the absolute limit for a good pole vaulter. No one would ever clear a bar 15 feet off the ground.

Then someone discovered that a fiberglass pole gave a little higher lift to the athlete. Poof! The legendary 15-foot barrier vanished. One Polish pole vaulter (No, that isn't a play on words or an oxymoron) has cleared 18'11¾". No doubt, the new goal is 20 feet.

Experts were wrong about the limits for high jumpers. Equally wrong about the limits for pole vaulters. Maybe they are just as wrong about what they think your limits are.

Maybe you are, too!

Stand Up to Them!

"Nobody has ever done it!" might mean nobody will . . . until you do it!

A Statue With Limitations

One hundred thousand dollars seemed like an obscene price. Even for the tallest structure of its kind in the world in those days. Especially with the U.S. economy slogging through a deep depression in the mid-1870s. One newspaper editorial insisted that the proposed project was preposterous:

**"almost too fantastic and
too poetic ever to be realized."**

An editorial in *The New York Times* took a tougher stance. It called into question the patriotism of anyone who would venture to support the project:

**"No true patriot can support such expenditures
. . . in the present state of our finances."**

Unfortunately, the original cost estimate wasn't half-right. When the project was completed the total cost was just shy of $250,000.

French citizens had shouldered the expense of creating a splendid monument. But New Yorkers had to bear the cost of site development and constructing its pedestal. These were the "expenditures" that editorial writers considered exorbitant.

Each piece of this massive structure was numbered and labeled in preparation for shipment from Paris. It took more than 200 wooden crates to pack all of the pieces. These were loaded on 70 railway cars in Paris. They traveled by rail to a port where they were transferred to a French ship for the transatlantic voyage. When the ship arrived in New York harbor with its priceless cargo, it was greeted with great fanfare.

But it was greeted by a major setback, too. Donations for building the pedestal had trickled in. Critics of the project reveled in the fundraising problems. They poked fun at the proposed statue, lampooning it as a wrinkled old crone lacking a pedestal to stand on.

Despite the critics, the funds were raised. Ten long months after the monument arrived, the pedestal was constructed. The statue now had a leg to stand on.

Three hundred separate copper pieces were riveted together to construct the statue. It weighed 225 tons (equal to 450,000 pounds). Standing 151 feet tall from toe to torch, it rises 305 feet above the harbor on its pedestal. It was, and still is, an impressive monument.

One index finger of the statue is eight feet long. The head measures ten feet from ear to ear. Even the nose stretches four feet in length.

Was it worth $250,000 to build the pedestal for this glorious gift from the people of France? Who should we ask?

Should we ask the millions of immigrants who sailed past the Statue of Liberty to disembark at Ellis Island and begin their new life in "the land of the free?" Or should we ask the soldiers and sailors who sailed past "Lady Liberty" into New York harbor after risking their lives overseas? How do you think they would vote?

Or should we ask the millions of visitors, both foreign and domestic, who visit this splendid shrine to freedom every year? What do you think? Was it worth such an extravagant expenditure more than a century ago? What is "Lady Liberty" worth to you?

What "true patriot" doesn't regard the Statue of Liberty as the greatest symbol of freedom that the world has ever known?

Stand Up to Them!

**Those who have nothing good to say
would be better off not to say it.**

A Capital Idea

On July 15, 1790, Congress approved the move to a new "Federal City" to be constructed on the banks of the Potomac. A sleepy little town in Maryland was convinced that it would be the site of the new nation's capital. Acting upon this expectation, the town fathers made grand plans to be:

**"the great, glittering capital
of a new and growing nation."**

This small town expanded its main street so that it was one hundred feet wide. They knew that the new capital would need an avenue for the ceremonial processions of kings and princes who would visit.

Two centuries later, Williamsport, Maryland, has been described as "a remote and tiny village with one enormously wide street." Great expectations drove its leaders down the wrong road.

Stand Up to Them!

**Not every road paved by good intentions
will turn out to be a capital idea**

Too Little For Too Much

In 1803, it was not the name of a state. It was the name that the French had given an unmanned, undefended territory that comprised one-third of North America. And it was for sale. But some thought the price was outrageous. One critic wrote:

"We are to give money of which we have too little for land of which we already have too much."

Seven of the thirty-one United States Senators voted "No!" to ratifying the treaty that would cement the deal. "We don't want it!" they insisted. New England states feared that the new states carved from this "unexplored empire" would upset the balance of power in the United States. It was the size of four or five European nations.

New Englanders feared becoming a minority partner in the Federal government. Some opponents to the treaty advocated that the New England states should secede from the union. Others complained that this territory was:

"A great waste, a wilderness unpeopled with any beings except wolves and wandering Indians ...."

This territory had been the property of France. But after the "Seven Years War"—which we call the "French and Indian Wars"—ended in 1763, France deeded it to Spain. In 1800, a reluctant King Charles IV of Spain gave the territory back to France under the terms of a new treaty. He wanted to appease Napoleon.

Thomas Jefferson, the 3rd president of the United States, heard about this new deal between Napoleon and Spain. Knowing Napoleon might be in a mood to strike a deal, Jefferson sent precise instructions to Robert Livingston, his ambassaor in France. Livingston had authority to offer $10 million for New Orleans and

Florida, or $7.5 million for New Orleans alone. New Orleans was the strategic gateway to the "Mighty Mississippi."

Napoleon, hoping to be crowned emperor of France, knew that his arch-enemy, the British, controlled the seas. With its naval power, England could seize any French territory they wanted. So, it was in Napoleon's interest to sell his huge North American territory to the United States, another of Britain's enemies. He would get whatever price he could as long as he still had it to sell.

Talleyrand was Napoleon's agent handling the sale. One of his peers, who despised him, snorted, "For money Talleyrand would sell his soul." When Livingston called on Napoleon's minister of foreign affairs, Talleyrand asked the American, "What would you give for the *whole* of Louisiana?"

Caught off guard, Livingston countered with an offer of $4 million. It was an insult! The Louisiana territory encompassed 828,000 square miles. But Napoleon absorbed the insult. He knew that he had to sell Louisiana or he would lose it to the British. One month later, he agreed to sell it for $15 million.

No one had any idea exactly what the United States had purchased. The wording of the treaty was vague, so the boundaries of the territory were not clear. Jefferson ordered a survey of it. He commissioned Meriweather Lewis, his private secretary, and William Clark, a veteran of several Indian campaigns, to go on an expedition.

They enlisted the help of a pregnant 16-year-old Indian girl named Sacajawea and her French-Canadian husband as their guides. She was an exquisite choice. When they encountered an angry Soshone Indian chief, Sacajawea intervened. Lewis and Clark discovered later that the chief was her brother.

Eighteen long months after the expedition left St. Louis, it reached the Pacific Ocean. Now the United States had a good survey of the territory it had purchased. All of the land between the "Mighty Mississippi" and the Rocky Mountains.

Jefferson's "Louisiana Purchase" more than doubled the size of the United States. A 140% increase to be exact. Thirteen states would be carved out of this territory. If you were to average out the cost, it would amount to less than four cents an acre! Can you imagine almost a quarter of the Senate voting, "No!" to what was "the greatest real estate deal in history?"

Stand Up to Them!

**People who vote against you today
may discover they voted wrong tomorrow.**

Memory-Gate

If you bought a computer back in the early 1980s, you may have had a machine with 256K (256 kilobytes) of memory. Or, if you were a gutsy pioneer, you might have dared to buy a Commodore 64 (with only 64 kilobytes).

In the new millennium, however, memory is measured in megabytes. Each megabyte equals 1000 kilobytes. For today's cyber warriors, 64 *megabytes* of memory is pint-sized. That's why this comment in the December 1996 edition of *Windows* Magazine hit a funny bone:

"640K ought to be enough for anybody."

Somebody must have had to dig in the archives to find that silly prediction made in the Stone Age of personal computing in 1981. And it was one of the great pioneers of the computer industry who insisted that 640K was plenty.

Wouldn't you guess that Bill Gates is delighted that he was wrong about that arbitrary limit? Microsoft, owned by Gates, has reaped the benefits of making people forget about memory barriers.

Stand Up to Them!

People might be convinced that enough is enough, until you demonstrate that even more is not enough.

"A Woman Won't Do."
But Did!

When Miss Roberts considered running for office, she hit the "glass ceiling." A party chairman, desperate to find a candidate for a House seat in Parliament, asked friends for suggestions. "Well, there's a young woman, Margaret Roberts, that you might look at," one offered. Not thrilled by the suggestion, the party chair scoffed,

"I don't think a woman would do at all."

It wasn't likely the first time that Miss Roberts heard those words. And it wouldn't be the last. She failed to get elected in her first two attempts. While on a short list to be her party's candidate at least five other times, she was never chosen. Probably because some party hack did not think "a woman would do at all." As she remembered:

> I would be short-listed for the seat, would make what was generally acknowledged to be a good speech – and then the questions would begin. With my family commitments, would I have time enough for the constituency? Did I realize how much being a Member would keep me away from home? Might it not be better to wait a year or two before trying to get into the House? And sometimes more bluntly still: did I really think that I could fulfill my duties as a mother with young children to look after and as an MP? What I resented, however, was that beneath some of the criticism I detected a feeling that the House was not really the right place for a woman anyway.

Eventually, she was chosen by the party faithful to run for an empty seat. She won. Sixteen years later, she was the first English woman to serve as the leader of a political party. She was elected to the highest office in the land four years later.

What was the secret to her magnificent success? Her ability to outlast her critics:

> I wouldn't be worth my salt, if I weren't attracting some controversy and criticism. Everyone in the world who has done something in life has attracted criticism. If your main objective was, 'Please, I just want to be liked and have no criticism,' you would end up by doing nothing in this world.

No wonder she was Europe's first female prime minister. And the only Prime Minister in Britain to win three consecutive terms in the 20th century. Both times she was re-elected in landslide victories. She left office after serving eleven and a half years, longer than any P.M. since 1827.

Maybe if that party chairman years earlier had known what the Soviets discovered (they nicknamed her "the Iron Lady"), he would never have dared to say, "I don't think a woman would do at all." But Margaret Thatcher did "do"—all the way to Number 10 Downing Street! Three times no less!

Stand Up to Them!

**What will never do are predictions like,
"You won't do!" or "You can't do it!"**

"Cut It Out!"

You've seen the bumper sticker, "If you can read this, thank a teacher," haven't you? Do you think this one might catch on: "If you have had surgery, thank an anesthesiologist." Probably not. But can you imagine going "under the knife" without getting "knocked out"?

Years ago you wouldn't have had any choice. People couldn't imagine the possibility of dozing in surgery in those days:

> **"The abolishment of pain in surgery is a chimera. It is absurd to go on seeking it today. Knife and pain are two words in surgery that must forever be associated in the consciousness of the patient. To this compulsory combination we shall have to adjust ourselves."**

I wonder what this "expert" would say, if he could witness laser surgery. But, years before lasers, pain was eradicated during surgery by the use of *anesthesia* (derived from a Greek word meaning "without feeling").

William Morton, a dentist, was the first to demonstrate that general anesthesia was possible. Before that, the only relief a patient could hope for was a "Ho, ho, ho and a bottle of rum."

Dr. Morton used *ether* for a tooth extraction on September 30, 1846. Then, in October, he anesthetized a patient with *ether* to remove a neck tumor at Massachusetts General Hospital. Another surgeon, Dr. Crawford Long, had used *ether* on his patients as early as 1842. But practicing in rural Georgia he did not publish his findings until 1849. So Dr. Morton is hailed as the father of general anesthesia.

But, it was another physician, Dr. Alfred Velpeau, who pontificated about "knife and pain" forever joined at the hip in the operating room. His painful prediction was made in 1839. Three years later *ether* was used by a rural Georgia surgeon to abolish pain in surgery.

Stand Up to Them!

Future generations may find "Absolutely absurd!" words like, "That's absurd!" muttered in the present.

Two Mistakes In One Sentence

A young lady returned home thrilled with a contract offer from Berry Gordy Enterprises. Her father put his foot down. He did not share her enthusiasm for the opportunity.

> **"Daughter, you are not signing any contract with anyone's fly-by-night enterprise."**

Very few fathers want to watch their lovely daughters go into show business. This dad was no different. He planned to have his daughter go to college and do something "sensible" with her life. He did not see any future in Berry Gordy Enterprises. That was his second mistake.

"What was his first mistake?" you ask. Attempting to keep his daughter out of show business. But more about that in a minute.

Berry Gordy did not inspire a father's confidence. He dropped out of high school at sixteen to box as a featherweight. With 15 amateur bouts under his belt, he swore, "I'm not going to work on a job for eight hours a day 'cause that ain't where it's at." But neither was boxing. It was followed by a tour of duty in the army.

Berry returned to his hometown at the ripe-old age of 24. He was ready to settle down. Borrowing $700 from "Pops," he opened his own record store. Known as the 3-D Record Mart, it specialized in jazz. Like his boxing career, it was short-lived. Two years after the store opened, Berry closed the doors.

This young upstart, who pledged that he would never "work on a job for eight hours a day," wound up sticking hubcaps on Fords on the assembly line. As you might have guessed, he didn't keep that job either.

Through connections he had in the music business, Berry got hooked up with a group called the *Matadors*. "Never heard of them," you say. Yes, you have! Berry Gordy helped the group and their 18-year-old singer/songwriter Smokey Robinson produce their first hit single as *The Miracles*.

Berry owned his own record label. It was very successful, thanks to recording stars like *The Supremes*, Stevie Wonder, Marvin Gaye, the *Temptations*, and the *Jackson Five*. By 1982, Motown Records, Berry's company, boasted revenues of $104 million. He had recorded 110 number one hits. Fly-by-night, indeed!

Oh, yes, and the father who put his foot down against his daughter going into show business, was Fred Ross. His daughter, Diana, and her trio, the *Supremes*, helped put Berry Gordy Enterprises over the top.

Stand Up to Them!

**Some "fly-by-night" enterprises
have soared to great heights.**

"Curses! Fooled Again!"

As the chairman of the Joint Chiefs of Staff, the old salt was known for speaking his mind. But even Admiral Leahy must have regretted the day that he told the President:

"That is the biggest fool thing we have ever done."

He offered his "expert" opinion about a new weapon. It would "never go off," he argued. There was no doubt in his mind about that.

It was only used twice. But not because it failed to "go off". It wasn't needed after the second time that it exploded.

At Hiroshima, 78,000 Japanese citizens died when the atomic bomb was dropped. Three days later another was dropped on Nagasaki, killing 25,000 more.

People can, and will, debate whether those bombs should have been dropped. But who would dare take Admiral Leahy's side of the question as to whether the bomb would work. "The bomb will never go off," he said, "and I speak as an expert in explosives."

Stand Up to Them!

Who is the bigger fool?" Is it the person who says, "It can't be done!" or the one who dares to get it done?

"Operation Dustrag"

Her first semester in college caused a rude awakening. She had been a good student in high school. Now, achieving a C- was an effort. With her disappointing report card in hand, she made an appointment to see her academic advisor. During their brief conversation, the counselor asked the obligatory question, "What do you want to do with your life?"

She wasn't sheepish about her answer. "I want to be a writer," she gushed. Her advisor took one look at her grades and shook his head,

"Don't even try it."

Can you blame him? She was struggling to make the grade in her freshman English composition class. Even worse, when she submitted articles to the campus newspaper, they were rejected. She didn't write well. Her hopes of getting a job on campus as a reporter were dashed.

But she wanted to be a writer. Go figure. Taking a job at a department store, she edited the employee newsletter. She got positive feedback. People thought that the features she wrote were funny. They loved her sense of humor.

She wrote a few features for another campus paper. One of the editors for the campus magazine, *The Exponent*, was enthusiastic about her work. "You can write!" he cheered. "You can write!"

She wrote a column for a local paper. But "Operation Dustrag" never caught on. A humorous glimpse at housewives and housework was not the ticket for her. Yet! She was married and children were an imminent threat. Her writing career had to be put on hold so she could raise a family.

One day her passion for newsprint returned. She knocked on the door of the editor of her local newspaper. He glanced at samples of several humorous pieces that she had written. Though he was tempted to say, "No!" he decided to give her a break. A weekly column was born.

Her weekly feature got the attention of the editor of the other city paper that had featured "Operation Dustrag." Years later, she recalled: "I didn't know him. We had never met, but if there is one person in this world who is responsible for what I have done, it's that man."

He offered to have her write three columns a week for the paper's editorial page. Three weeks later he submitted several of her columns to Tom Dorsey at Newsday Syndicate in New York. Dorsey was ecstatic. "She was in tune with suburban women all over the country," he recognized.

"At Wit's End," her column, was featured in 500 newspapers across the country within five years. Then came the books. They were runaway best-sellers.

The Grass Is Always Greener Over the Septic Tank sold 500,000 hardcover copies in the mid-70s. *If Life Is a Bowl of Cherries, What Am I Doing in the Pits?* followed a year and one-half later. It sold 700,000 in hardcover. Her seventh book, *Motherhood: The Second Oldest Profession,* sold almost a million copies in hardcover.

This "Socrates of the Ironing Board" left behind countless homespun one-liners that have outlived her. Like: "Never lend your car to anyone to whom you have given birth." Or: "A friend is someone who doesn't go on a diet when you're fat."

Erma Bombeck was told not to try her hand at writing. She put that hand to good use, don't you think?

Stand Up to Them!

**You might need to try harder when
they tell you, "Don't try it!"**

A Looney Idea?

President Kennedy trumpeted the goal of putting a man on the moon during his inaugural address in 1961. "Before this decade is out!" he proposed. What a joke! It seemed as unlikely as, well. . . a man on the moon. Kennedy sounded like, pardon the pun, a raving lunatic.

Critics had a field day. Few were as polite, however, as this editorial comment from one particular trade publication:

> **"The odds are now that the United States will not be able to honor the 1970 manned-lunar-landing date set by Mr. Kennedy."**

To be honest, the technology needed to send a man to the moon did not exist in 1961. Kennedy had set a goal, which, in Star Trek-ese, was, "to boldly go where no man had gone before."

Grave challenges faced NASA scientists at every turn. Complex issues related to trajectory and velocity had to be solved. Mathematical equations had to be formulated to tackle the logistical problems of space travel. Engineering problems demanded creative solutions.

Booster rockets needed to be capable of traveling 250,000 miles from earth. Spacesuits had to be able handle the fluctuations in temperature on the moon (200° F. during the day; -200° F. at night). Even a lunar module had to be developed that enabled the astronauts to descend from the orbiting spacecraft to the surface of the moon. It had to be able to launch from the moon, too, so that it could rendezvous with the spacecraft once again.

To further complicate the matter, NASA suffered a horrible setback in January 1967, when flames erupted in an oxygen-rich spacecraft during a countdown. Three astronauts died in that disaster.

Kennedy's pipe-dream appeared to die on that launch pad with them.

But on July 20, 1969, Neil Armstrong took his infamous, "One small step for a man, one giant leap for mankind." All those nay-sayers had to swallow hard. Especially the magazine that insisted a "manned-lunar-landing" would never happen by Kennedy's self-imposed deadline.

Would you like to know which magazine made that dire prediction? What a laugh! It wasn't *Time*, or *Newsweek*. It was the April 20, 1964, edition of the *New Scientist*.

Stand Up to Them!

Those who say "The odds are against you!"
will sound very odd to those who see you succeed.

Slim's Chances

New York hotel magnate Raymond Orteig offered a $25,000 prize to the first person to accomplish the feat. It was a daredevil's stunt. Six men died trying it. "Slim," the son of a former Congressman, intended to do it. He approached the managing editor of the St. Louis *Post Dispatch* for financial backing. He was turned down cold:

"We have our reputation to consider. We couldn't possibly be associated with such a venture!"

Others protested, "The risks are too high." But several businessmen in St. Louis chose to sponsor his attempt to compete for the $25,000 prize. Critics put pressure on Slim's sponsors to talk him out of this hair-brained scheme. They feared that he was throwing his life away. Reporters branded him "the Flyin' Fool" and "the Flyin' Kid."

One plane had flown all the way across the Atlantic Ocean. But that flight had an entire crew, and they had to make two fuel stops in their navy seaplane. No one had ever flown from New York to Paris non-stop.

Orteig's $25,000 prize had never been claimed. Not after a number of years. Most were convinced that it never would be. No one would dare to fly it solo. Except Slim. He was a parachute jumper and a stunt pilot. A *bona fide* daredevil. After a year of intensive training at the army flying school in Texas, he had flown a mail route between St. Louis and Chicago. He did it solo. He preferred to travel that way.

Not every "flyboy" was thrilled to see "the Flyin' Fool" take up the challenge. A number of airline executives cornered Harry Bruno, Slim's public relations rep. They pulled no punches:

"Bruno, why are you mixed up in this suicidal stunt flying? Four men lost in four weeks—you are sending men to their deaths. You'll ruin aviation in America."

The plane was nothing fancy. It was a single-engine, single wing, less than 28 feet long. It boasted an instrument panel almost as primitive as one in a 1927 automobile. It did not have a radio, and there was no sextant to help him navigate. He would be flying blind.

Slim tested his aircraft by making a record-breaking flight from New York to California. But on his trans-Atlantic flight, he would be carrying extra fuel in a special compartment in the nose of the plane. An experienced pilot observed that, "very little room had been left in the cockpit for the pilot." After giving the plane "the once over" he concluded, "This fellow will never make it. He's doomed."

On May 20, 1927, a skinny, 25-year-old stunt pilot took off from a primitive, muddy runway on Long Island in a drizzle. He barely cleared the telephone lines because of the weight of all of the extra fuel he was carrying in the nose of the plane.

Slim had packed five sandwiches for the trip, and he took a quart of water to drink. But he only ate one sandwich and half of another during the trip. Most of the time he was fighting fatigue and battling doubts about his chances of success.

In New York City, 40,000 boxing fans were asked to stand and pray for this young daredevil that night. In London, Berlin, and Amsterdam, all of the stock exchanges interrupted their trading sessions with updates. All that could be reported was that there was nothing to report. There had been no word from Slim. How could there be? He didn't have a radio.

At sunset on that second night, everyone in Paris who owned an automobile was asked to drive to the landing strip at *Le Bourget*. They lined up along the runway. Their headlights would be the only beacon that the young pilot would have in the fog—if he survived the transatlantic flight.

After 33 hours and 29 minutes of grueling mid-air torture, Slim touched down in Paris. Tens of thousands of Parisians mobbed *The Spirit of St. Louis* and its gutsy pilot, "Lucky Lindy." As he stepped from the plane, he proclaimed, "I am Charles Lindbergh."

One U.S. newspaper gloated that this non-stop transatlantic flight was, "the greatest feat of a solitary man in the records of the human race." Back in New York, "Slim" received a hero's welcome—a ticker-tape parade up Broadway. In the nation's capital, he was awarded the Congressional Medal of Honor.

Lindbergh would no longer be jeered as "the Flyin' Fool." Now that he had conquered "impossible" odds, he was romanticized as the "Lone Eagle." Not that Lindbergh was in a class by himself. But it sure didn't take long to call the roll. Six other men had died trying what he succeeded in doing.

Can you imagine how that poor newspaper man in St. Louis must have felt? He missed out on a chance to be part of the story of a lifetime. Lindbergh's solo transatlantic flight was the one "venture" that he would regret not being associated with.

Stand Up to Them!

**Don't listen to the prophets of doom
or you will be doomed to quit trying.**

Wrong By A Mile

In 1954, medical journals featured articles that asserted that the human body was not designed to achieve one particular milestone.

**Medical experts argued that the body could not
endure the wear and tear this feat would require.**

Then someone did it. In 1954! Over the next two years, 213 others did it! Today, every serious contender has to do it, too. Even in high school track.

"What was this cherished milestone," you ask? Would you believe that medical experts insisted that it was impossible for a human to run a four-minute mile?

"History repeats itself," Woody Allen quipped, "It has to. Nobody listens the first time around." Maybe he's right. You have to wonder if the "experts" will ever listen to the lessons the past teach us.

Medical experts better be listening, that's for sure. After all, it was a young medical student, Roger Bannister, who was the first to break a four-minute mile in 1954.

Stand Up to Them!

**"Experts" may tell you, "It can't be done!"
But don't expect them to explain how you did it.**

"Throwing Peas Against A Wall"

Have you ever worried that the light at the end of the tunnel might be the headlight of an on-coming train? If so, then you can identify with Manya. As a young woman, she wrote to a friend about the bleak prospects for her future:

> My plans for the future? I have none, or rather they are so commonplace and simple that they are not worth talking about. I mean to get through as well as I can, and when I can do no more, say farewell to this base world. The loss will be small, and regret for me will be short—as short as for so many others.

Could you blame her? Born in Poland, her family suffered under the harsh rule of the Russians. Her father, a professor, was demoted when Russians were installed in most of the teaching posts in Poland. He endured a salary cut and lost 30,000 rubles in an investment that went sour. Plus, Manya's mother died when she was eleven.

Through it all, Manya excelled as a student. Not bad, considering the Russian superintendent took an instant dislike to her. She complained about the girl's "scornful smile" and fussed about her rebellious locks. Manya had curly hair that she tried to braid. Out of frustration, the superintendent groaned to a colleague one day:

"It's no use talking to her—it's just like throwing peas against a wall."

Manya graduated from the Russian school at age 16. She was awarded a gold medal, despite the misgivings of the superintendent. Polish women weren't allowed to enroll in the Soviet-controlled universities so she and her sister struck a bargain. Manya would support her sister while she attended medical school in Paris. Her sister agreed to return the favor.

For six years Manya provided support to her sister by serving as a governess to a wealthy family. They were difficult years. She didn't read any "serious books" and was "sunk in the darkest stupidity." Manya hit bottom, intellectually. She confessed to a cousin, "I can't believe geometry or algebra ever existed. I have completely forgotten them."

Finally, it was her turn to attend the Sorbonne in Paris. She lived alone, scraping by on a diet of bread, fruit, and hot chocolate. Manya graduated with the equivalent of a master's degree in physics and mathematics. About that time, she met Pierre, her future husband and research partner. Joining him in the lab, she engaged in research on the project that earned her a doctorate.

"It was judged to be the greatest scientific contribution ever made by a doctoral candidate," noted her biographer. In 1903, as a reward for their research, she and her husband received the Nobel Prize for physics. Three years later, however, dark days returned. A loaded cargo wagon ran over Pierre and killed him as he crossed a Paris street.

Manya persevered, recovering from the shock of Pierre's tragic death. Appointed to be the chair in physics in Pierre's place, she was the first woman to serve as a professor at the Sorbonne in its glorious 650 year history.

In 1910, Manya isolated pure radium. This led to her being awarded a second Nobel prize. She has the distinction of being the first and only woman to win two Nobel prizes, one in physics and one in chemistry.

Her laboratory was her life. "I don't know," she confided to her sister in 1927, "whether I could live without the laboratory." Ironically, it was her work in the laboratory that killed her. Constant exposure to radioactive materials contributed to Madame Curie's death from leukemia.

Have you ever seen the film *Madame Curie*? In it, Pierre became frustrated after their 487th experiment on radioactive materials had failed. He threw up his hands in despair and cried, "It can't be done; it can't be done! Maybe in a hundred years it can be done, but never in our lifetime."

Madame Curie's response was priceless: "If it takes a hundred years it will be a pity, but I dare not do less than work for it so long as I have life."

Granted, that particular conversation was probably the fabrication of a Hollywood script writer. But it was an accurate portrayal of the determination of the little Polish girl who refused to give up, even in her darkest hours.

She did not lead an easy life. And she did not die a pleasant death. But her accomplishments are certainly "worth talking about," contrary to what she, herself, once predicted.

Stand Up to Them!

The world may act like it can do without you until you show that it can't afford to lose you.

Five Is Enough!

How many different personal computers have you owned or used? Don't forget to count laptops and PDAs. How many did you come up with? Could you count them on one hand? Or was it more than a half dozen?

Can you imagine an expert going public with this prediction in 1948? He insisted that one computer was all that would ever be needed. Not one for every home or office. Just one computer! It "could solve all the important scientific problems in the world involving scientific calculations," he surmised.

Later, this genius hedged his bet. He whipped out a calculator and multiplied his original estimate by *five*:

"I think there is a world market for about five computers."

Do you remember the days of punch cards? Computers were the size of small bedrooms in those days. It might have been feasible to agree with him, then. Since the development of the personal computer in the early 1980s, however, one more expert opinion has bit the dust.

Today, everyone is chattering about DOS or Windows (or the "Mac"), e-mail, the Internet, CD-ROMs, laptops, and laser printers. Mouse pads and keyboards have replaced pens and paper. Typewriters are antiques. Computers are nearly omnipresent. Cameras, watches, and thousands of other electronic devices are virtual mini-computers because of the development of the microchip.

Companies that did not exist twenty years ago are now household names and they have been a stockholder's dream come true. Who hasn't heard of Microsoft, Apple Computer, Intel, America Online, and Hewlett-Packard? Those are the best known. But there are many more where they came from.

Consider Bill Gates, too. Yes, he has been branded "the silicon bully." And his company has been sued by the Justice Department. But he has name recognition around the globe and earned the title, "youngest billionaire in the history of America." All because personal computers have multiplied like rabbits.

Can there be any question, then, that Thomas Watson, Sr., jumped the gun in 1943? He never envisioned today's "typewriter of choice," the personal computer.

Funny thing is, Mr. Watson, Sr., was the chairman of "Big Blue," better known as IBM. It was his son, Tom Watson, Jr., who teamed up with Bill Gates and Microsoft in the early 1980s to spearhead the computer revolution.

Stand Up to Them!

It is extremely difficult for others to measure your future potential in the present tense.

Everyone Can't Own One

The Literary Digest reported on the "latest" invention. It characterized this contraption as "a luxury for the wealthy." Not that the editors considered it worth much fanfare. They were confident in their grim assessment:

> **. . . although its price will probably fall in the future, it will never, of course, come into as common use as the bicycle.**

Can you blame the authors of this distinguished publication? You could dress this "baby" up, but you couldn't take it out. It was loud and obnoxious, a public nuisance. Who would have dreamed that the "horseless carriage" would catch on? Well...not counting those hundreds of millions (or is it billions) of people who have bought one, that is.

You do see more bikes on the road than cars these days, don't you?

Yeah, right!

Stand Up to Them!

What will those who know, "It will never catch on!" say when they see that "it" actually has caught on?

What A Wild Idea!

A lone senator took to "the well" of the United States Senate and offered a dazzling objection to what he perceived to be just one more "pork-barrel" project. To propose this hare-brained idea, he deplored:

> **" . . . manifests a wild spirit of adventure which I never expected to hear broached in the Senate of the United States."**

Normally, citizens appreciate politicians cutting out "the pork." But, in 1843, if a majority of his peers had voted with him, it would have been a serious blow to the western frontier. Instead, the Federal Government agreed to pay Leland Stanford's company a staggering $16,000 per mile to blast and chop through 300 ice-and-snow-bound miles in the Rockies.

Altogether, Stanford's company was responsible for constructing 690 miles of rail, most of it through mountainous terrain. Meanwhile, another company, the Union Pacific, was busy laying 1,085 feet of rail across much more level terrain. Each company worked with crews of 10,000 men performing hard labor for low wages.

Stanford's company, the Central Pacific, had another obstacle to overcome. It had to transport all of its supplies, including the locomotives, around Cape Horn at the tip of South America. This entailed a voyage of 12,000 miles aboard relatively swift Clipper ships.

Since each mile of track laid required 40 railroad cars full of rail, timber, food, and fuel, you can imagine the logistical headaches. Ten spikes were driven into each rail and they needed 400 rails per mile of track.

On May 10, 1869, an enthusiastic crowd gathered for an extraordinary ceremony. Some dignitary swung the silver hammer and drove a symbolic golden spike into the last railroad tie of the Transcontinental Railway.

Two locomotives inched toward each other, one from the west and one from the east. They bumped cowcatchers and the news was telegraphed by Western Union to both coasts: "U.S. annexed." East and west were able to meet at last. That "wild spirit" to which one senator loudly objected in 1843, was the construction of "a railroad to the western shore of this continent."

Stand Up to Them!

**If others don't expect it to happen,
you may need to make it happen.**

A "Joke" Gets The Last Laugh

She was known at Hitsville, a local recording studio, as "that secretary who thinks she can sing." She and three of her high school friends had formed a little singing group they called the *Primettes*. One day she approached the lead singer, Florence, and notified her that she wanted to sing the lead on certain songs. Florence snubbed her, objecting:

"But you ain't a lead singer."

Mary, another member of the group recalled, "Whenever she would insist on a lead and then sing it, we would sort of look at each other and try not to laugh. She had this weird little whiny sound."

Her producer at Hitsville shared the same concern. He wondered whether she had a singing voice, or simply a high-pitched whine. He remarked to one of his future singing sensations:

**"Be honest with me. She sounds
kinda whiny, huh? Kinda weird?"**

Her producer panicked when he heard that she had dropped out of her vocal music class at school. She was about to get a "D". He tried to convince a friend in the music business to manage this young girl and her singing group, the *Primettes*. His friend thumbed his nose at the opportunity. "No one wanted to get involved with a kid who sings through her nose," he lamented regarding his decision.

Another female lead singer from a rival group, the *Marvalettes*—who already had a hit song, "Please Mr. Postman"—spotted this young lady's grandiose ambition: "American bandstand was her dream. She wanted to be on the show more than anything. We all thought,

'Surely she must be joking! and I think we started laughing. But, believe me, she was quite serious.'

Yes, she was! But the *Primettes* would never be famous. Not as a quartet. Or by that name. One of the girls got pregnant and dropped out of the group. The other three never did get their big break on Dick Clark's American Bandstand. Their debut was on Dick Clark's annual "Calvalcade of Stars" summer tour starring Gene Pitney, The *Shirelles*, and Brenda Holloway. They were billed as one of the "others."

However, by the end of that summer tour, their first hit single catapulted them to Number One on the Billboard charts. By the time the summer tour ended, they were the act that got the top billing. Dick Clark had secured the services of "one of the most successful female singing trios of all time" for a paltry $600 a week.

But the girls did not achieve success as the *Primettes*. Their producer hated that name. They were forced to choose a different name from a list generated by someone at Hitsville. One of the girls preferred one particular name on the make-shift list. But the young lady with the "whiny" voice objected to it. She said that it sounded like a name for a male group.

While the trio argued over which name they preferred, a secretary at Hitsville took matters into her own hands. She chose a name from the list and typed it on the recording contract.

These poor young women were stuck with a name they didn't choose. They were known as *The Supremes*. But they chose to make the most of it, didn't they? As did the high school girl with the "whiny" voice.

Can you imagine? Diana Ross would have received a "D" in vocal music, if she hadn't dropped the class.

Stand Up to Them!

**Those who said, "You ain't got it!"
may never get it. . . . Got it?**

"A Passing Fancy"
In The Present Tense

In 1912, Arthur Brisbane made a bold prediction in the *Chicago Herald-Record*. He deplored the latest innovation in the performing arts community:

**They "are just a passing fancy and
aren't worth comment in this newspaper."**

Today, every newspaper features large, bold ads for these artistic achievements that Mr. Brisbane dismissed as unworthy of his time or attention. By the way, good luck trying to locate a copy of the *Chicago Herald-Record* these days. It has passed away.

However, audiences all over the globe fancy "motion pictures." Movies generate huge advertising revenues and endless copy for every newspaper in the country. Plus, movie stars grace the covers of magazines and can, single-handedly, sell gossip sheets like the *Star* and the *National Enquirer*.

Stand Up to Them!

**Be sure to wave when you are passing by
those who thought you were "a passing fancy."**

Couldn't Sell Worth A Dime

Frank was a terrible salesman. His boss cut his pay from $10 a week to $8.50. Summoning him to the cellar of the store for a heartless-to-heart talk, his boss explained,

"I've got boys earning six dollars a week who sell more stuff than you."

It was a huge blow to the young man's ego. "I became convinced I was not fitted for mercantile life," Frank admitted. His health collapsed a short time later and he was out of work for eighteen months.

While he was recuperating, Frank got married. His father-in-law sold him six acres with a house on it in exchange for a $300 promissory note. It was a tremendous bargain, even in those days. But Frank was no farmer.

After trying his hand at farming for a year, he jumped at the chance to get back into retail. His ex-boss had sold the store and the new owners offered him $10 a week to work for them. Then business dropped off, and his new boss cut him back to $8.50 a week again. Just before his wife gave birth to a baby girl.

One month later Frank's fertile mind gave birth to the idea that changed his life. He overheard someone boasting about stores in certain cities that had experimented with five-cent counters. He convinced his boss to give it a try.

They bought $100 worth of cheap goods and set them up on a special counter. Every item on that counter was priced to sell for a nickel. On the very first day they sold all of them.

Five-cent fever was spreading and Frank caught the bug. Many stores tried it for a month or two, until the novelty wore off. But Frank dreamed of operating a store where everything was sold for a nickel. He approached one of his uncles for financial backing. Frank never forgot what his uncle told him:

"He said I was very foolish to think of such a thing, and that if I knew which side my bread was buttered, I'd hang onto my $8.50 job."

It was the dumbest advice his uncle had ever given. Passing up the opportunity to invest in Frank's future turned out to be the worst decision that his uncle ever made. Fortunately, Frank's boss allowed him to buy $300 worth of items on credit, with Frank's father co-signing the note.

His first store in Utica, New York, closed after a few months. But his lease on the small storefront was month-to-month, so he moved on. Next stop, Lancaster, Pennsylvania. Two months later, he had a branch store in Harrisburg. Then one more in Scranton.

His brother suggested they add a second line of goods priced at ten cents an item. With that the "5 & 10 Cent Store" was born. A "browsers wanted" policy was adopted. By 1886, seven years after striking out to make his fortune in nickels and dimes, Frank had seven stores. By 1895, there were 28 stores, and, by the turn of the century, he had 59 stores in operation.

As the 20th century dawned, Frank's stores were selling more than $5 million in merchandise. Five years later sales had tripled. In 1911, he merged his 319 five-and-dime stores with five other rival companies to create a huge conglomerate. These 596 stores, with sales topping a million dollars a week, operated under the banner of the F.W. Woolworth Company.

One potential investor, who had refused to loan Frank money, found a colorful way of quantifying his foolish decision. "As far as I can figure," he quipped, "every word I used in turning Woolworth down cost me about a million dollars."

Stand Up to Them!

You can make your critics look like fools for concluding that you were too foolish.

No Time Like The Present

Don't you think that a Wall Street broker should be able to spot a great investment opportunity when he sees one? But nobody's perfect, right?

However, John Wesley Hanes, of C.D. Barney & Co.—a precursor to Smith Barney—was no ordinary financier. He would serve as FDR's Under-Secretary of the Treasury. You would think that when he spoke, two young Yale grads should have been listening. As they outlined their ambitious plans he exploded:

> **"You would be crazy to try to buck the *Literary Digest*. . . . Forget it and save your money."**

But they couldn't forget it. And neither will you. These two ambitious young men quit their day-jobs to pursue their dream. Their boss was confident that they would be back. He told them that they could have their old jobs back, if things didn't work out.

They had no money. So, naturally, they sought to raise the $250,000 in start-up capital that they figured they needed. Then reality set in. After hearing "No!" repeatedly, they reduced their goal to $100,000. "We had to . . . peddle stock," one of them recalled, "to our friends and our *friends'* friends." He recalled that experience as "the hardest year of my life." But after ten months of fund-raising, they settled for less than $87,000 as working capital.

One of the core beliefs of this new enterprise was that "people in America are, for the most part, poorly informed." Noting that there were one million people in the United States with a college education they decided to make "every one of these 1,000,000" their target audience.

It was a herculean task to create the first weekly "news-magazine" that "aimed to serve the modern necessity of keeping people informed." When the first issue (dated March 3, 1923) appeared on news-stands, it was 32 pages long. Critics panned it as "a thin, unimpressive little magazine selling for the relatively high price of fifteen cents."

But, it made a huge impression on a news-hungry public. In its sixth year of publication, the average number of copies sold in the fourth quarter was 23,000. After that sales skyrocketed.

Meanwhile, the *Literary Digest* that John Wesley Hanes prized so highly began to die a slow, agonizing death. It had been the brainchild of Funk and Wagnalls, the encyclopedia people. The *Digest* was an institution in the late 19th and early 20th centuries. In the early 1920's it had a circulation of more than one million readers. Its famous straw votes predicted the results of presidential elections.

Then the editors of the *Digest* made a very poor, and very public prediction regarding the 1936 election. They predicted Alf Landon (who?) would defeat FDR and his "New Deal" by a landslide. They were right about the landslide. But it was Roosevelt who slaughtered Landon 523 to 8 in the Electoral College. Two years later, the *Literary Digest* was put out of its misery.

People who invested in the early days of this new weekly news-magazine became wealthy. That included the circulation manager. In the magazine's seventh year he sold RKO stock that he had inherited from his father. He did so against the advice of his stockbroker. RKO was worth $35 a share at the time.

With those proceeds, he bought 550 shares of stock in the news-magazine, priced at $360 a share. Two years later, even after the stock market crashed in 1929, his new stock was worth $1,000 a share. RKO stock, meanwhile, had tumbled to a pitiful seventy-five cents a share.

Doesn't that make you wonder about John Wesley Hanes, the Wall Street broker, who refused to invest in *Time* magazine when it was valued at $25 per share? How often do you think he kicked himself, realizing that he was the one who was "crazy" for not investing in the company when it was dirt cheap?

In its seventh year of operation, Hanes did purchase 100 shares at $360 a share. It was still a great buy, but not as spectacular as the bargain he turned down the first time. His *Time*-ing was a little off.

Stand Up to Them!

**Anybody who is "Anybody"
has been called crazy by somebody.**

"You Don't Know Anything!"

Kay's mother never wanted to have children. When Kay was born, her mother described her as a "wretched little object, made even more hideous by abrasions on her poor little temple made by the forceps."

After Kay got married, her mother's scorn continued. She told her daughter that she could never be anything other than a housewife.

One day Kay wandered in while her husband and her mother were engaged in a deep conversation. Her mother objected to the interruption:

**"Pardon us, dear, but we are having
an intellectual discussion."**

You get the implication, don't you? Kay certainly did. "This is way out of your league, my dear. You aren't bright enough to discuss such weighty matters. Your place is with the children."

Years later, after Kay had distinguished herself as a savvy businesswoman, her mother continued to put her down. During a lunch meeting, an architect mentioned something noteworthy, and Kay admitted, "I didn't know that." Her mother grabbed that moment by the throat and squeezed:

**"What's surprising about that?
You've never known anything."**

Would you believe that Kay's mother was revered as a top-notch educator? Maybe she was one. But she had a great deal to learn about being a parent, didn't she?

Tragically, Kay's husband committed suicide. He had been the president of the company that Kay's father had rescued from bankruptcy. She stepped in to take the reigns, which was completely out of character for her.

She startled the board of directors (all men) when she informed them, "This has been, this is, and this will continue to be a family operation. There is another generation coming, and we intend to turn the paper over to them." You could have knocked those guys over with a feather.

But Kay was wrong about one thing. Her son, the "next generation," had to wait many years after he had graduated from Harvard to take the helm. It was his mother who led the *Washington Post* and *Newsweek* magazine into the "information age." Katherine Graham, contrary to what her mother thought, was fully capable of "an intellectual discussion." She out-smarted all of them.

Stand Up to Them!

People who think you are incapable will be stunned at how capable you turn out to be.

Drilled Out, But Driven On

Word was out that there were two openings on the varsity squad. If he could join the team immediately, this high school sophomore figured, he could qualify to play in the state tournament. He already had the advantage of playing as a starting point guard on the junior varsity squad.

So, he and a friend tried out for the vacancies on the varsity team. They ran drills and did everything they could to showcase their talents. When the coaches posted the alphabetical listing of varsity players he was disappointed to find that his name wasn't on it.

He did not make the cut. But his friend, six-foot-five Leroy Smith, did make the team.

How could he have failed to make the team? Sure, he wasn't as tall as Leroy. But he was a good point guard, wasn't he? Maybe not.

He did go to the regional tournament. But not as a varsity player. He was the team's equipment manager. This dejected sophomore watched the games from the bench, handing towels to the players after every buzzer.

This disappointment was a wake-up call for him. Prior to failing to make the varsity squad, he had focused more of his time and energy on baseball. "I was actually a better baseball player than I was a basketball player when I was growing up," he admits today. "I always thought I'd be a professional baseball player."

But now he turned his attention to the basketball court. Almost non-stop. He vowed that he would never warm the bench again. "I made up my mind right then and there that this would never happen to me again. From that point on, I began working harder than ever on my basketball skills." At the start of the next season he was 5 inches taller and a star on the varsity basketball team.

His varsity coach was the first to dismiss this young man's talents. But he wasn't the last. Street and Smith publish a list of the top 300 high school prospects every year. They did not include this future hall-of-famer in their list the year he graduated.

Isn't that ironic? He is a basketball legend. Many basketball fans salute Michael Jordan as "Mr. Basketball." Few would dispute the claim. He led the Chicago Bulls to five NBA National Championships in seven years.

How would you like to be known as the high school basketball coach who chose Leroy Smith over "Air" Jordan?

Stand Up to Them!

**Though you are not good enough today,
you can still be the best you can be someday.**

"Now I Know My ABCs"

Most parents wonder how their children will turn out. Young Tommy must have been a constant source of concern for his parents. He didn't learn to read and write at a normal age.

Tommy could not recite the alphabet until he was nine years old. Reading had to wait until he was twelve.

He was a frail little guy. By his own admission, he was "always a slow fellow in mental development—long a child, longer a diffident [timid] youth." Tommy was, by all appearances, a "professional student." He struggled to find his niche. His father warned him of the danger of becoming an idle dreamer:

"Do not allow yourself, then, to feed on dreams— daydreams though they may be."

After pursuing several courses of study at many fine colleges and universities, he became a professor at a women's college when he was 29 years old. It was a miserable experience for Tommy and he quit after three years. But he persevered in his chosen profession. In his early thirties this carefree young man was "becoming a self-confident (mayhap a self-assertive) man."

This growing sense of confidence, and his perseverance, paid off. He was chosen to be the President of Princeton University a dozen years later. Time had toughened his hide, but preserved his tender heart. During one traumatic period in his tenure at Princeton, he dug in his heels, refusing to resign.

"The heavier the storm, the tighter I will sit," he resolved. Timid little Tommy had blossomed into one of the most influential leaders of his generation.

He left Princeton and was elected to Congress for one term. Next, he was elected governor of New Jersey. But there was more to come. Much, much more. Thomas Woodrow Wilson, a "late bloomer," blossomed into the 28th president of these United States.

Stand Up to Them!

**Don't let them count you out
just because you don't count yet!**

"Us Four And No More"

We don't like people who stick their nose into other people's business, do we? How often have you heard, "Mind your own business!"? But there are times when you can't afford to keep to yourself. Especially on the world stage. One world leader found that out the hard way, when he boasted . . .

"We seek no part in directing the destinies of the world."

World War II proved how wrong he was. Then the Cold War reinforced the same lesson. Since then the United States has either been applauded or denigrated for acting as the world's policeman. Pundits labeled the 20th century "the American century," because "we" couldn't keep to ourselves.

President Warren G. Harding failed to comprehend America's "manifest destiny" in 1921. He died during his third year in office. Harding played no part in "directing the destinies of the world." But his successors sure did.

Isn't it interesting that the man who wanted us to keep our collective nose to ourselves had people sticking their nose into his business? Harding presided over a scandal-ridden administration. Maybe the worst in the 20th century.

Stand Up to Them!

Those who fail to mind their own business, should try harder to mind their tongues.

Bank on It!

Bill and his partner were the proud owners of a new A&W root beer stand in Washington, D.C. Hoping to borrow $1,500 so that he and his new bride could go on a nice honeymoon, Bill approached the bank.

Mr. Bigelow, the banker, gave him a kindly smile and pointed out that his root beer stand was thousands of miles away. Besides, the banker assured him, the equipment wasn't enough collateral.

Bill owed a bank in Utah $1,500. In 1927 that was not chump change. He had been fortunate to get the original loan, considering the enormous distance between Washington, D.C. and Utah. Who could blame the banker for being reluctant to trust this young upstart with an additional $1,500?

Under their franchise agreement, Bill and his partner couldn't sell food. They could only dispense root beer at their nine-seat road-side stand. Profit margins weren't bad, but it was a seasonal business. Ice-cold frosty mugs made it a nice summertime business. But that season only lasted four months.

There were significant risks to consider. By all appearances the banker was making a smart business decision. But as we all know, appearances can be deceiving.

It was Bill who convinced the people at A&W to allow him to sell food at his root beer stand. He was the only franchisee they allowed to do it. And that was just the beginning. Soon he had two root beer stands, which he transformed into *Hot Shoppes*. Then three. Then dozens and dozens.

He built a hotel in D.C. in the mid-1950's. Then he built dozens and dozens of hotels, each more up-scale than the other. When he died in 1984, Bill left behind a company that had become "a world leader in lodging and food service." It employed 154,000 people and generated annual sales of over $4 billion.

How would you like to be known as the banker who refused J. Willard Marriott a loan because he didn't have enough collateral? You do recognize the name Marriott, don't you? As in, *Marriott Inns and Suites.*

Stand Up to Them!

**Those who turned you down should
watch for where you turn up next.**

Enough Already?

An executive with McGraw-Hill, the book publishers, went out on a limb when he made this grim economic forecast in a national trade publication:

> **As a nation we are already so rich that consumers are under no pressure of immediate necessity to buy a very large share—perhaps as much as 40%—of what is produced, and the pressure will get progressively less in the years ahead. But if consumers exercise their option not to buy a large share of what is produced, a great depression is not far behind.**

Translated into simple English, this gentleman predicted that American consumers had plenty of "stuff." They would have little reason to buy much else in the future. A full-scale depression was inevitable, as far as he was concerned.

Half a century later, his comments seem silly, don't they? When people don't think they need any more things, an advertising jingle assures them of something they need to buy. Think about how many radio and TV commercials, billboards, or glossy magazine ads you see on a daily basis. Talk about pressure to buy!

One study estimates that the average adult in the United States gets bombarded with 500 advertising messages every day. The average child, they insist, watches approximately 20,000 television commercials every year. By the time that child is 18 years of age, he or she has seen and heard approximately 1,800 *hours* of commercials. Once again, pressure to buy.

It is an advertiser's responsibility to generate a feeling of need in the mind of John and Jane Doe. Madison Avenue types have turned ordinary words into household brands. Take "Pride" and

"Joy," for example—two ordinary words that they transformed into trademarks.

No wonder the *faux pas* committed by the McGraw-Hill executive sounds so ridiculous today. Would you like to know what is most comical about his pessimistic forecast? It appeared in the October 24, 1955, edition of a magazine known as *Advertising Age*.

Can you imagine? This dire prediction about satisfied consumers appeared in a trade publication read by the very people who make sure that the pressure to "shop 'til you drop" will not get "progressively less in the years ahead."

Stand Up to Them!

Remember: the customer is always right!
Not the economic forecasters.

Wrong Degree but
the "Right Stuff"

He was a hillbilly from West Virginia. He didn't have the "right stuff" to be a test pilot. They were college graduates. Most had engineering degrees. He was thrilled to have a high school diploma—majoring in girls. As an assistant maintenance officer, it was his job to perform in-flight safety checks on planes that had been overhauled or repaired.

He did know how to put a plane through its paces. Other pilots dismissed him as a show-off. One test pilot did not mince words when he told him to his face:

"We weren't trained to do acrobatics. We're precision fliers. If I handed you a test card and told you to go test an airplane, you couldn't do it."

After World War II, the Army Air Corps developed the X-1 project. The goal was to fly a test plane past Mach 1—over 700 mph. It was a risky mission. Most scientists believed that at Mach 1 the shock waves would be so intense that an airplane would crack up in mid-flight.

The flight commanders in charge of the project reviewed 125 "jet jockeys" in the flight test division to pick just the right man for this assignment. They wanted "a pilot capable of doing extremely precise, scientific flying." They chose the West Virginia hillbilly.

On October 14, 1947, the X-1 was dropped like a bomb from a B-29 at 20,000 feet. When the experimental plane started into a stall, the gutsy pilot fought to stabilize it. Then he fired all four rocket chambers and the plane began to climb at .88 Mach. At 36,000 feet, he turned off two of the rocket chambers. Passing through 40,000 feet, he was climbing at .92 Mach.

Leveling off at 42,000 feet, with 30% of his fuel left, he fired the third rocket chamber again.

The X-1 reached .96 Mach. The faster it went, the smoother the ride was. Nobody expected that.

Suddenly the Mach needle went haywire. It tipped off the scale for about twenty seconds. When the engineers measured all of the flight data, they determined that the X-1 had flown at 1.07 Mach— 700 mph.

Believe it or not, the "hillbilly" had broken the sound barrier. He and his plane came back in one piece. He was the "precision flyer" who pulled off this high-risk mission. You have to admit that Chuck Yeager knew how to "test an airplane."

Stand Up to Them!

**If you listen to the people who say,
"You can't do it!", then you won't do it!**

On the Right Track

Like any normal red-blooded American boy, he dreamed of being "an athlete." His youthful ambition was simple. "I just wanted to be on any team," he explained. "If I couldn't be a pitcher, I'd play anywhere. If not baseball, any sport would do."

**As a ninth grader he decided to try out for track.
He didn't make the cut.**

To qualify for the track team, he had to run a quarter mile. When the gun sounded, he took the lead. Half-way around the track, however, he ran out of gas. He finished the race, but his time was not good enough to make the team.

However, the gangly 6'1" fifteen-year-old didn't take "No!" for an answer. He worked hard and made a name for himself running track. He competed in three different Olympic Games. Individually, or as a member of a relay team, he set *eight* world records in his running career.

But think of it. Jim Ryun, "Mr. Mile Run," failed to make his ninth-grade track team running the quarter mile. For him failure wasn't the end. It was a reason to begin again.

Stand Up to Them!

**Nobody will care what you couldn't do
once you do what only you can do!**

A Secret Weapon:
"No Alternative!"

Her mother had a blueprint for good Jewish girls from Milwaukee. Quit school, work as a clerk at a downtown store, and then "marry, marry, marry while quite young." Goldie recalled, "My mother didn't want me to have an education. She thought it was for men only."

There was only one problem. Goldie had other plans. She was about to enter the ninth grade. Her mother wanted her to drop out of school, but Goldie wanted to graduate from high school and go on to get a teaching degree. Her mother recommended secretarial school instead, warning:

"A clever girl you'll never be!"

Not true. She had to be clever just to survive. She ran away from home at 14 because her parents would not allow her to go to high school. Goldie moved out to Denver to live with her sister. But that did not work out. Goldie left after one year. With no money, no job and no place to stay, she was desperate.

She accepted an invitation to live with a couple who were dying from tuberculosis, a deadly and highly infectious disease. It wasn't an ideal arrangement. But Goldie couldn't afford to live anywhere else until she quit school and took a job. She found work in a laundry, earning half of what the men who worked there made.

It was a letter from her father that ended Goldie's three-year exile. He urged her to come back home and go to school. She graduated from high school and earned a degree at the Milwaukee Normal School for Teachers.

During that time she got active in politics. She married and persuaded her husband to move to Palestine and live in a kibbutz, a collective farm for Jewish refugees. The couple moved to Jerusalem where she was thrust into the heart of the Zionist cause to establish a Jewish state.

In May 1948, Goldie joined with other Zionists in signing the Israeli Declaration of Independence. She was elected to the Knesset (the Israeli parliament). She proved to be a "man's man" in a world of men. David Ben Gurion, the first prime minister of Israel, quipped that she was "the only *man* in my cabinet."

Some honored her as "the most important woman in the world" at the height of her political career. Others described her as "one of the most outstanding women of our century." Why? As the *New York Post* editorialized:

> Imagine an area of 8,000 square miles in all. Make it 270 miles long and seventy miles wide at its widest; border it on three sides with enemy nations, their armies totaling between 70,000 and 80,000 troops; place within it 6,000,000 people from more than 50 nations, whose last experience with self-rule dates back 1,887 years; sever its sea and air communications; sack its former government; give it a name; declare it independent—and you have the state of Israel, one minute past midnight, May 15, 1948.

Saudi Arabia's king threatened the state of Israel in its infancy. "With 50 million Arabs," he hinted, "what does it matter if we lose ten million to kill all the Jews?" Egyptian leaders boasted, "Within two weeks we will be in Tel Aviv."

But fifty-six years later, the nation of Israel persists. Thanks, in large part, to the *chutzpah* of a woman who defied all the odds. In 1969, Goldie assumed the role of interim prime minister. In

October of that year, she became the first and only woman to be elected Israel's prime minister.

It was on her watch that the Egyptians and Syrians staged a surprise attack on *Yom Kippur*, the Day of Atonement. Arab anti-tank and anti-aircraft missiles devastated Israeli ground and air forces. Jews in Israel faced the specter of a second holocaust.

Within a matter of days, the Israeli armies stemmed the attack. Then, in a strategic move, they advanced on the Suez Canal. Egypt's forces in the Sinai Peninsula were cut off from their supplies. No reinforcements could get through, either. They surrendered.

"I didn't know how we would make it," Goldie once said. "I only knew one thing, that we must. . . . We had a secret weapon: 'No alternative!'"

Anyone who watched Golda Meir ascend to prime minister of Israel knows that, contrary to what her mother said, she was quite "clever."

Stand Up to Them!

**Be more clever than your opponents and
you won't have to be the smartest of the bunch.**

A Wholesale Mistake

This new kid, fresh out of college, didn't exercise care in handling the paperwork after a sale. He screwed up some of the sales slips and had trouble manning the cash register. But he could sell. One of his general managers told him:

> **"I'd fire you if you weren't such a good salesman. Maybe you're just not cut out for retail."**

But the young man worked hard. At first he worked for others. Then he went into business for himself. When he started his own company, he had a tough time finding investors. Nobody wanted to invest in a new company with such radical, new approaches in the industry. It was too much of a gamble. He had to put up 95% of the money himself.

For twenty-five years his company ranked number one in the industry for the lowest ratio of expenses to sales. In other words, they controlled costs better than anyone else. But that wasn't his only key to success. He discovered that there was much more business in small-town America than anybody dared to dream.

He was asked in the early years, "How big do you want this company to be? What is your plan?" He replied that he could foresee adding one or two more locations to the five he already had, " . . . if we can grow with our own money."

Little did he know.

"With the possible exception of Henry Ford," Tom Peters (who knows *Excellence* when he sees it) championed this business owner as "the entrepreneur of the century." Even an arch-rival in business conceded, "He is the greatest businessman of this century."

What was his secret? He studied what everybody else did, stole their best ideas, and then made them even better.

In 1985, *Forbes* magazine trumpeted Sam Walton as "the richest man in America." He was worth $20-25 billion dollars. That's billion . . . with a "B!"

How did he make his astonishing fortune? In retail. Despite the fact that one of his early bosses questioned whether Sam was cut out for retail sales. His *Wal-Mart* is the largest retail company in the world, selling "for less."

Stand Up to Them!

**Don't cut them in on your success,
if they didn't think you were cut out for it.**

Time-Waster or Waste of Time?

Lee DeForest admitted that "theoretically and technically" this new concept "may be feasible" but:

" . . . commercially and financially I consider it an impossibility, a development of which we need waste little time dreaming."

One man's fiscal nightmare can become another man's commercial dream come true. Many, many people have made a good living—a very good living—off this venture that DeForest didn't think was a sound investment. Some have gotten very rich because of this clever invention.

DeForest thought this nifty appliance was a waste of time. Not so, from a marketing standpoint. But it has turned out to be a time-waster for many people—those who are its target market. You know, like couch potatoes.

Would you believe it? DeForest, who saw no future for TV in 1926, was a pioneer in the earliest days of radio broadcasting. He died in 1961, which means that he lived long enough to see how wrong he was. He was widely honored as the "father of radio" and the "grandfather of television."

Stand Up to Them!

Don't let yourself be found wrong when you were right all along.

A Dim-Witted Dumbbell

Her younger brother nicknamed her "Brian." It was a dubious put-down. "Brian" was the name of a dim-witted snail from a local children's TV program called *The Magic Roundabout*. This poor little girl took the put-down to heart and concluded:

> **"I wasn't good at anything. I felt hopeless, a drop-out. Brain the size of a pea – that's what I've got. I'm as thick as a plank."**

Her younger brother was very clever. She longed to be "as good as him in the schoolroom." But she never excelled academically. "Brian" failed all the exams at the all-girl school that she attended. Twice! It is one of life's great ironies that she began her career as a teacher's assistant.

When her mother packed her bags and abandoned the family, "Brian" was devastated. Nannies tried to take her mother's place. Most of them described the distraught little girl as "difficult" and "tricky" after her mother left. "She wasn't easy," one of them recalled. "Some children that young will do as they are told immediately, but she wouldn't, it was always a battle of wills. She was full of spirit."

Her parents' divorce took quite a toll on little "Brian." She was nursing deep emotional wounds from growing up in a broken home. She told another one of the nannies:

> **"I shall only get married when I am sure I am in love, so that we will never be divorced."**

Unfortunately, her romantic fantasies never materialized. Her public courtship with a noteworthy figure on the world stage led to "the wedding of the century." The whole world attended her wedding—thanks to the media coverage.

But thanks to that same media scrutiny, she endured a public and painful separation and divorce. Some have even blamed her death on an overly zealous press corps.

Little dim-witted "Brian," a quintessential ugly duckling, had grown into a glorious swan. After her untimely death, it was her younger brother who delivered an unforgettable eulogy to the "People's Princess." He remembered Princess Diana—little dim-witted "Brian"— as "the very essence of compassion, of duty, of style, of beauty."

Stand Up to Them!

**If you aren't good at much of anything,
don't conclude that you're good for nothing.**

A King-Sized Mistake

Columbia Records had heard about the brand new singing sensation. They expressed interest in buying out his contract. Sam Phillips, whose local company owned the singer's contract, offered to sell it for $20,000. The executive from Columbia was shocked:

"Forget it. No artist is worth that kind of money."

Then RCA came calling. Phillips was offered $35,000 to sell the contract to RCA. He could use the money to help promote the careers of some of the other half dozen performers that he had under contract.

Phillips decided to ask a friend for advice. He called Kemmons Wilson, the founder of Holiday Inn, and woke him from a dead sleep. Wilson was never one to hesitate in giving his opinion:

"$35,000 for a performer who is not even a professional? I'd sell that contract!"

No doubt that was the worst advice Kemmons Wilson ever dispensed. One year later, the young singer was a celebrity. One of his records sold 2 million copies. Another sold 3 million. Stores were selling $75,000 worth of the new star's records every day.

During that year alone, this singing sensation had six of RCA's all-time top 25 records. In less than three years, he released 14 consecutive records that each sold more than a million copies. In the years to come, 45 of his records would sell over a million copies each.

Again, one year after Columbia refused to buy his contract for $20,000, this singer starred in the first of his 33 films. By the time of his untimely death, 500 million copies of this singer's records had been sold. In the five days after his death, another 8 million of his records were sold. In fact, during the eleven months after his death, royalties from his movies and records earned an additional $5 million for his estate. It was more than he ever made in any one year during his spectacular 25 year career.

Can you imagine how many times executives at Columbia Records must have kicked themselves for saying "No!" to Elvis Presley's contract for a measly $20,000? "No artist," not even the future King of Rock 'n' Roll, "is worth that kind of money."

Yeah, right!

Stand Up to Them!

"It's not worth it!"
may not be worth saying.

Stuck on Stupid

Don't you hate it when you get stuck on stupid? It helps to remember that it happens to the best of us, not just the rest of us:

> **He ought to be in *The Guinness Book of World Records* for building one of his homes on somebody else's lot—TWICE.**

Yet this high school dropout, despite some costly blunders, was a very successful home builder. He became a millionaire building houses. But he amassed the bulk of his fortune elsewhere, building a different kind of company. A very successful company.

When he took his new company public half a dozen years later, he and his partners sold 120,000 shares of stock at $9.75 a share during the first day of trading. In time, the company was receiving 10,000 requests per year for new franchises.

His new company was conceived during a family vacation. He was irritated by the miserable conditions and hidden costs of motels all along their vacation route. Every motel charged two dollars extra for children and a dollar to rent a TV. Worse yet, the family had to hunt for a restaurant when they wanted something to eat.

Before they returned home, he told his wife that he was going into the motel business. Instead of building homes, he would build motels. But, in his motels, children would be allowed to stay for free. "How many of these motels are you going to build?" she asked. "Oh, about 400 ought to do it," he replied. She laughed. It did seem absurd in 1951.

An article in the *Wall Street Journal* estimated that there were roughly 20,000 roadside "lodgings" in the United States in the early fifties. Most of those were "unappetizing roadside camps," they noted.

In 1956, the Federal government passed a massive $76 billion federal highway program. This meant that more people would be venturing out on the road, needing a place to stay at night. At one point, the new company was adding a new motel every two and a half days and a new room ever fifteen minutes. By the early 1970s, his motels had three times as many rooms as their main competitors.

It was the architect who did the sketches for Kemmons Wilson's first motel that gave the company its name. "I saw Bing Crosby's *Holiday Inn* on television last night," he ventured.

"It's a great name," Wilson agreed. "We'll use it."

So now you know the origin of all those functional Holiday Inns. They were built by the same man who built homes on the wrong property—TWICE.

Stand Up to Them!

**Don't make the mistake of giving up
every time you make a mistake.**

Hazardous to Your Health?

You probably have one in your home. Maybe more than one. But you may never have considered the "health risks" this common household fixture could represent for your family. In the 1840s, "experts" in the U.S. denounced it:

> **"It is an Epicurean innovation from England designed to corrupt the democratic simplicity of the Republic."**

Loosely translated, the argument was that this new invention would double people's pleasure and double the nation's trouble.

Medical experts couldn't resist throwing in their two cents worth. They warned against this "innovation" as "a producer of rheumatic fevers, inflammatory lungs and all zymotic [contagious] diseases."

So what was this common household fixture that could introduce such disastrous social and medical complications? Would you believe it was the bathtub? Did you have any idea how risky a soak in the tub could be?

Stand Up to Them!

**They might be dead certain this time,
but they have been dead wrong before.**

The "Unrepentant Bachelor" Who Repented

H. L. Mencken, the editor of the *American Mercury* until 1933, was known in his day as "America's most unrepentant bachelor." He was also dubbed, "The Antichrist of Baltimore." His rabid cynicism sank its nasty fangs into the soft flesh of tradition:

> **"Marriage is a wonderful institution. But who would want to live in an institution?"**

Ouch!

But he was also a hard-core chauvinist. Can you imagine him getting away with this barb in a politically-correct polite society today? "The only really happy folk are married women and single men," he sniped.

Or imagine him getting away with this one these days?

> **"Bachelors know more about women than married men. If they didn't, they'd be married too."**

Then in 1930, the 50 year-old bachelor shocked his readers and fans. He got married! One headline read, "Mencken . . . Capitulates To Cupid." His devotees were confused and outraged. They felt betrayed.

He gloated. "Getting married," he quipped, "like getting hanged, is a great deal less dreadful than it has been made out."

Why did he get married, people wondered? His glib response was, "I formerly was not as wise as I am now."

H. L. and his wife, Sara, lived "happily ever after" for five brief, blissful years as her fragile health deteriorated. When she died in May 1935, he suffered a loss deeper than words could express.

"When I married Sara the doctors said she would not live more than three years," he admitted to a friend. "Actually she lived five, so I had two more years of happiness than I had any right to expect."

Mencken would later admit, "I was fifty-five years old before I envied anyone, and then it was not so much for what others had as for what I had lost." The unrepentant bachelor had repented.

Stand Up to Them!

**Even when you are wrong
you can still make it right!**

A "Metal Monster"

When the Centennial Committee unveiled their proposal, it was heaped with scorn. This was not the way to commemorate one hundred years of freedom, people objected.

Many of the citizens of this noble world capital were deeply offended by the steel pyramid selected for their "Centennial Exposition." They showed profound contempt for this "useless and monstrous" monument that they dubbed it "the Tower of Babel." It was mercilessly criticized as

"a superb hardware shop" and a "truly tragic lamppost . . . a distress symbol of shipwreck and despair."

Accusations flew fast and furious. "It would rape the glorious architecture of this fair city," some argued. "It would humiliate the glorious monuments that surrounded it," they charged. It would prove to be "an unavoidable and tormenting nightmare."

Those who felt such righteous indignation argued, "Everyone feels it, everyone says it, everyone is profoundly saddened by it, and we are only a weak echo of public opinion so legitimately alarmed."

They equated the project with "administrative devastation and the vandalism of industry." And they predicted, "For the next twenty years we will see cast over the entire city . . . the odious shadow of the odious column of bolted metal."

What critics imagined as a "dizzily ridiculous tower" became a technological masterpiece and an architectural marvel by the turn of the century. The 984-foot structure was twice as high as the dome of St. Peter's Basilica in Rome or the Great Pyramid in Egypt.

It was the tallest man-made structure in the world until 1929, when the 1046-foot Chrysler Building was completed in New York. More than one hundred different plans had been submitted to the Centennial Committee. However, it was the design of a world-renowned bridge engineer, "a magician of iron," that was ultimately selected for the Exposition.

Today this "metal monster" is one of the world's most recognizable landmarks. Brazen caricatures of it like "this tall, skinny pyramid of iron ladders," or "this giant and disgraceful skeleton," sound silly today. It is now one of the premier tourist attractions in the world. This "awful" tower, the Eiffel Tower, once skewered, is now adored.

Stand Up to Them!

What some find tasteless at first, may stand the taste-test of time.

Not "Big League" Material?

No words sting a ballplayer's ears more than these: "I'm sending you down to the minors." After playing for a big league club, it's a giant step backwards to be shipped down to one of the farm teams.

For one 19-year-old rookie, it signaled the end of his career. Back in the minors, he was mired in an 0 for 21 slump (no hits in 21 at-bats). He called his dad and pleaded with him to understand why he was about to abandon his baseball dream:

> **"I'm not hitting, Dad. I just can't play anymore. I tried as hard as I could. And what for? Where am I headed? I'm telling you, it's no use and that's all there is to it."**

His dad drove through the night to confront his 19-year-old son. When his son fussed about throwing in the towel, this wise father growled, "I'm gonna' pack your stuff, that's what I'm gonna do. You can go back and work in the mines like me!"

As he threw his son's dirty clothes and socks into a suitcase, he muttered, "I thought I raised a man."

Reverse psychology triumphed again. His boy promised to give it another chance. During his next forty games in the minor leagues, the 19-year-old belted 11 home runs, drove in 50 RBIs, and hit .361. He was on fire . . . and on his way back to the big leagues by the end of August.

However, his father never saw his son develop into a baseball legend—a future Hall of Famer. In early May of the following year, his dad died. By the end of that season the twenty-year-old phenom had belted 21 home runs. One of them was a tape-measure shot that sailed 565 feet.

Four years later, he accomplished one of baseball's rarest feats. He won the triple crown, hitting more home runs (52), getting more RBI's (130), and batting for a higher average (.353) than anyone else in the league. He was the obvious choice for the American League's MVP award.

In his career, he led the American League in home runs four times. He retired with 536 career home runs, all in Yankee pin-stripes. Thanks in large part to him, the "Bronx Bombers" played in 12 different World Series during his legendary 18-year major league career.

When he retired in 1968, there was no doubt that the Yankees would retire his number 7. The 19-year-old who didn't think he could play anymore was one of the most popular players in the game. The rookie who wondered, "Where am I headed?" would end up in Cooperstown, in baseball's coveted Hall of Fame.

When a teenager named Mickey Mantle told his dad, "It's no use and that's all there is to it," that wasn't all there was to it. As his teammate and Yankee class clown Yogi Berra used to say, "It ain't over 'til it's over."

Stand Up to Them!

**Everyone has doubts about success,
but the "stars" play through their doubts.**

Crazy Like a Fox

People in the industry thought he was "a crazy man." Summing up the popular sentiment, another industry executive explained,

"Most people thought he was nuts."

A fellow millionaire and business associate tried to prevent his crazy friend from committing financial suicide. "I tried to talk him out of doing it, because I was afraid he'd go under. I was also not convinced that he could do it." Years later, that same business associate admitted, "It was the best piece of advice he ever said no to."

This crazy fool was risking his entire fortune on an enterprise that scoffers ridiculed as

"the Chicken Noodle Network."

Insiders had their own nickname for the new startup. They called it the "Chaos News Network" because of all the bugs that had to be worked out. Their boss had earned his nickname because he was always shooting off his mouth. People chuckled about the man they called "the Mouth of the South."

Through its coverage of the Falklands War, the *Challenger* disaster, the TWA hijacking, Tiananmen Square, the collapse of the Berlin Wall, the Anita Hill/Clarence Thomas debacle and the Gulf War, the "Chicken Noodle Network" earned global respect.

Herbert Schlosser, the former president of NBC, argues that this "crazy" fool happens to be one of the three most important men in the history of T.V. He is a television tycoon, a multi-billionaire who appears on everyone's short list of the world's richest men.

Heralded as "half visionary, half crackpot," this ingenious fool gambled everything on his Cable News Network, better known as CNN. Ted Turner's gamble paid off—BIG! He has given a billion dollars from the profits of his cable networks to a United Nations charity. That's a huge batch of Chicken Noodle Soup for the soul.

Stand Up to Them!

**"It can't be done!" might be translated,
"We don't know how to do it . . . yet!"**

A "Dandy" Insult

Enemy troops made up the song. They sang it for the same reason that a football player engages in "trash talk" . . .to harass and intimidate.

> **They sang it to insult and mock their foes who wore no uniforms and lacked military precision and drill.**

But their little ditty failed to have the intended result. It provoked a response, but not the one they wanted. Their foe adopted the song and sang it with pride. What was supposed to be an insult, turned into a badge of honor.

Even the title was supposed to be insulting. "Yankee" referred to a New England country bumpkin. A hick. "Doodle" equaled a simpleton, or a silly fool. Those pitiful colonists in the American Revolution seized upon the British put-down and set themselves free from its sting. It was a "dandy" way to turn an insult into an incentive.

Stand Up to Them!

Keep in mind that "trash talk" should be deposited in File 13.

"Too Late" Too Soon

Unemployed and in strange surroundings, he tried to find work doing what he had always dreamed of doing. He knocked on the doors of studios all over Los Angeles. The answer was always the same: "No openings." He was young and inexperienced . . . and unnecessary.

His brother suggested that he should go back to the cartoon business.

"No, I'm too late. I should have started six years ago. I don't see how I can top those New York boys now."

Who could blame him? He had dabbled in the cartoon business back in Kansas City. Clients rarely paid him for the work that he did and he ended up declaring bankruptcy. He wanted to escape from the cartoon business. So he decided to leave K.C. and make a fresh start in L.A.

To raise money for a one-way ticket to California, he had gone door-to-door photographing babies. Then he sold his camera. But, after arriving at his destination, doors were slammed in his face. Besides, California was a long way from New York, where the latest and greatest cartoonists exercised their creative juices.

Reality set in. He owed his uncle $5 a week for room and board. Unable to pay the tab, he had to borrow money from his brother. His uncle nagged him about having no job and no prospects. In desperation, he listened to his brother's advice and gave the cartoon business one last shot.

He wrote an ambitious letter to a cartoon distributor in New York with a proposal for a cartoon series called *Alice's Wonderland*. His big break came by way of a telegram. The distributor in New York accepted his proposal with this offer: "Will pay fifteen hundred each negative for first six and to show my good faith will pay full amount on each of these six immediately on delivery of negative."

Alice's Wonderland was only the beginning. Soon the young cartoonist created two of his most enduring characters: a mouse he named Mickey and a duck he called Donald.

Building on his success, he created a fantasy land amusement park, which opened in 1955. Critics christened it "an amusement supermarket." Endless streams of kids, and their parents, however, choose to call it "Fun!"

Walt Disney could have given up. He almost did. But billions of people around the globe, young and old, are very thankful that he did not. We now live in a Disney world.

Stand Up to Them!

**You may regret that you didn't start sooner.
But that doesn't stop you from starting today.**

Getaway or "Gotcha!"

A popular magazine was offering suggestions for people who needed to get away. One of their vacation suggestions, in hindsight, turned out to be ludicrous. Here is what that magazine recommended:

"And for the tourist who really wants to get away from it all we recommend safaris in . . ."

They advocated a specific third-world country by name. It is that *name* that makes the magazine's suggestion sound ridiculous to those of us who hear about it today.

Events transpired to make this the one spot no one would have singled out as the place to go "to get away from it all." In fact, it was not a country that *any* Americans wanted to visit for any reason. Especially young men who had just turned 18 and had to register with the Selective Service.

How would you like to be known as the *Newsweek* reporter who prescribed a safari in Vietnam in the 1960s to the tourist who wanted to get away from it all?

Stand Up to Them!

**Everybody makes mistakes.
Try not to make yours in print.**

From Supergeek To Supermodel

Nobody in grade school likes to be known as "the brain" or "the geek." A high IQ can be a great liability at that age. One woman, who had to grapple with those insults, recalls that she thought of herself as an "übergeek" (or "supergeek"). As a teenager, she remembers:

"I was tall, unbearably skinny, wore thick glasses and had no sense of myself as a female."

She had a high IQ and "was predisposed to do technical things," she once told an interviewer. A chemical engineer, a mathematician, or a lawyer were her prospective careers.

No boy in her high school showed any interest in her. She was not asked to go to her high school prom. Her sister, Kelly, recalls that any boys that came to their house were there to see her, not the übergeek.

"It was me they came to see. She was always too busy with her head in a book. She was the ugly duckling. I was the beauty."

When she was fifteen, this "übergeek" began taking college courses part-time. She was bored with high school and needed a greater challenge. But then she was always advanced for her age. "I was like 40 at birth," she admitted in one interview. "When I wasn't even a year old I spoke, I was potty-trained, I walked and talked . . . I was a very intense, weird kid . . . everything I did and said made everybody uncomfortable."

But the "übergeek" began to take an interest in her appearance. The former "ugly duckling" transformed herself into a lovely swan. On a trip to New York City over Christmas break, she met Eileen Ford of the Ford Modeling Agency. Ford found her appearance intriguing and enlisted her as a model. While she dabbled in modeling, this young lady pursued her real interest— acting. She married a Hollywood producer and appeared in a number of, what she now describes as, "knucklehead B movies."

Though her marriage failed, her growing reputation as a sex symbol caused her acting career to rocket into the stratosphere.

Whatever else you may think of Sharon Stone today, it's doubtful that you would describe her as an "übergeek."

Stand Up to Them!

**What would you call those who insist,
"You're a loser!" after you become a winner?**

Bad Lyrics, Tough Tune, Hit Song

You already know that you can't please all of the people all of the time. But sometimes you can't please most of the people some of the time. Even when it comes to a song that is a fan favorite.

Some people complain that the song is too tough to sing. Some think the lyrics are antiquated. Others grouse that it is too militant.

Step back into the corridors of history a moment and refresh your memory. This song originated when there were storm clouds on the horizon. It was birthed while the smoke from enemy artillery swirled above an American port.

Dr. William Beanes, an elderly physician, had been taken prisoner by the British. His friend, a Maryland attorney, was asked to negotiate his release. The attorney boarded an enemy ship in the harbor to intervene on behalf of the old doctor. His request was granted, but the two Americans were not allowed to leave the British ship until the next morning.

During the night, the ship attacked a fort near Baltimore. The two men watched helplessly, pacing the deck, as the British bombarded the fort through the night. Their spirits were refreshed in the morning when they spied the fort's American flag flapping in the breeze.

When they were safe on shore, the attorney checked into a hotel in Baltimore for the night. There he composed a poem re-enacting the attack on Fort McHenry. His poem was printed the next day on a handbill and distributed throughout the city of Baltimore. It bore the title, "Defense of Fort McHenry."

One month later, the title was changed and the poem was set to the melody of an eighteenth-century tune from the British pubs—"To

Anacreon in Heaven." Many people do complain that the tune is tough to sing, but don't let that throw you. The tune is here to stay.

During the Civil War, the "Yankees" in the Union Army adopted the song. By 1895, army regulations required the song to be played whenever the American flag was being lowered. Then in 1904, the Secretary of the Navy ordered that it be played at morning and evening colors.

John Philip Sousa, best-known for his dramatic, patriotic marches, composed the official arrangement of the song for the military. But you might be surprised to learn this. It was not until 1931 that Congress voted to adopt "The Star-Spangled Banner" as our national anthem.

Yes, the words are antiquated. Yes, the tune is a bit difficult to sing. But as long as the sight of an American flag flapping in the breeze inspires a patriotic fervor, Francis Scott Key's rendition will continue to hit a nerve. Key, that attorney from Maryland, was inspired by "Old Glory" on that fateful morning after the British attack on one of our ports.

Ordinary Americans rekindled their love affair with the Stars and Stripes after a more recent attack on another of our port cities. All those emotions we experienced after September 11, 2001, gave us a fresh connection to the sentiments Key expressed two centuries ago. Times change, but life's raw experiences build bridges into the past.

Stand Up to Them!

People who gripe about you today might be singing your praises someday.

It Will Drive You "Nuts!"

What David Frost said about television applies just as well to radio. It permits you "to be entertained in your living room by people you wouldn't have in your home."

Media critics abound today. But can you imagine someone who had never heard a radio and had never seen a TV offering this brisk warning?

> **"Suppose someone invented an instrument, a convenient little talking tube which, say, could be heard over the whole land . . . I wonder if the police would not forbid it, fearing that the whole country would become mentally deranged if it were used."**

That great Dane, Soren Kierkegaard (1813-55), would probably be chagrined to hear what people are allowed to say and sing on that "little talking tube" today.

Stand Up to Them!

**Some who can see can't really see
because they don't have enough vision.**

A "Silly" Mistake

If you discovered a "mistake" by accident, would you be able to find a use for it? Peter Hodgson did in 1949. He stopped by to see a client, Ruth Fallgatter, the owner of a toy store in New Haven, Connecticut. While there, Ruth showed him an unusual substance that a friend had given to her.

Her friend, James Wright, a chemical engineer at General Electric, had created it. He stumbled upon this substance while working with various silicon compounds. It was a good "mistake."

General Electric saw no value in marketing this substance. They were looking for a new source of rubber. This was not it!

Ruth Fallgatter, the toy shop proprietor, couldn't see any value in fooling around with this substance either. She was hunting for new toys for the adult market. This wasn't one of them.

Hodgson, who did market analysis, was intrigued by Wright's new substance. He designed a creative package for the substance and convinced Doubleday to display it in their bookstores.

Did it appeal to adults? You bet! One of Doubleday's managers told Hodgson that it was "the biggest thing in the shops since *Forever Amber* and *Peyton Place*. Don't forget, this was circa 1950.

There was one common complaint, however. This gooey substance got stuck in people's hair and on their blue jeans. Hodgson had the "stuff" modified so that it didn't stick to anything or leave any stains.

So, did it sell? Did it sell! Thirty-two million packages of this new toy were sold in the first five years that it was on the market. Kids love it, too. Not just in the United States or in Europe, either. Sales were brisk in third-world markets like India and South Africa, too.

For Hodgson, it proved to be a $5 million per year bonanza. With the addition of a manufacturing plant in Frankfort, Germany, sales rose to $7 million a year.

GE made a big mistake when it dismissed James Wright's little "mistake." It proved to be an imaginative little toy. It could be stretched into any shape, like clay. You could mold it and stretch it into various shapes. Or you could bounce it like a ball. If you pressed it against an image on a page, it made an impression of that image. It was very versatile.

Hodgson had labeled the substance "gooey gupp" when he saw it in Ruth Fallgatter's store. Fortunately, that goofy name did not stick. But neither did the substance, once Peter made a few cosmetic changes.

But the name "Silly Putty" did stick—although "Silly Putty" did not stick to anything else. Oh, do you remember the creative package that Hodgson designed? It was a colorful plastic egg.

Stand Up to Them!

**Your critics won't see your potential.
But the key question is, "Can you?"**

Put-Down But Not Put Away

His *magnum opus* was not a run-away best-seller. How could it be with a title like, *Mathematical Principles of Natural Philosophy*? Voltaire, the cynical French philosopher, groused:

"This crazy mathematician will not have twenty followers in his lifetime."

Another critic was less kind. He accused the mathematician of having a "deranged poetical fancy."

Voltaire was right about one thing. This "crazy mathematician" lived another forty years after his book was published. His converts at the time of his death numbered less than a dozen.

All of this hub-bub seems amusing now. Very few people today have read or even seen a copy of Isaac Newton's *Mathematical Principles of Natural Philosophy*. But 99.9% of us accept its basic tenet—the law of gravity.

Who's crazy now?

Stand Up to Them!

Don't worry about how few are following today, if you are leading the way into tomorrow.

Multiply Your Best Guess by Five

Some people can't see the bird in their hands. Forget about the two in the bush. One young inventor had that problem. He didn't have a clue how valuable his new gadget was. He underestimated what it was worth.

One interested party asked him to name his price. He said he needed some time to think that over. When he rehearsed the conversation with his wife, she recommended that he should offer to sell it for $20,000.

"Twenty thousand dollars!" he barked. "I don't want to scare him to death."

His wife gave him an out. Just in case that figure set off alarm bells. "You could always say, 'Joking aside, Mr. Eckert, what do you think it's worth?'"

All night that figure of $20,000 danced in his head. If he could get that much for his little invention, he would pay off his debts and outfit a little laboratory. "It would make me the happiest man in the world," he reasoned.

When he visited Mr. Eckert the next day, Eckert asked him to name his price. Eckert knew that his company, the Western Union Telegraph Company, could put the young inventor's gadget to good use.

Everything in the young man wanted to shout, "Twenty thousand!" But the words wouldn't come out. He didn't have the nerve to ask for that much money. While he hesitated, Eckert threw out a proposal of his own:

"How about a hundred thousand dollars?"

The young inventor's knees almost buckled. Eckert's proposal was *five* times the amount he was too bashful to request! What would he do with that much money?

That thought scared him. He might kick back and take it easy, if he got a "mountain of money" like that in one lump sum.

"If you'll pay it in seventeen annual installments instead of all at once, I'll accept it," he countered. Mr. Eckert, as you can imagine, was delighted to accept those terms.

"Why did the young inventor suggest 17 years?" you ask. Thomas Edison knew that a patent lasted seventeen years. He wanted a guaranteed income for the life of the patent.

Of course, it didn't take Western Union anywhere near that long to install Edison's "stock ticker" in every bank and stockbroker's office in the country. Can you imagine? Edison could have held for more, and Mr. Eckert would have been happy to pay it.

Stand Up to Them!

**Don't sell yourself short.
You are in this for the long haul!**

"Box Office Poison"

It was a terrible discovery that destroyed a "most wonderful childhood." Thirteen-year-old Kathy was the one who found her brother hanging by a curtain tied from a beam in the ceiling in the bathroom. The *Hartford Courant* splashed this headline on the front page:

DR. _____'s SON, 15, HANGS HIMSELF WHILE VISITING IN NEW YORK — DEAD BODY SWINGING FROM CURTAIN. FOUND BY SISTER IN HOME OF AUNT — DESPONDENCY SUSPECTED.

This horrible tragedy had a devastating effect on poor little Kathy. She found herself battling depression. Her grades suffered as a result, and she felt awkward around other kids. Noticing her rapid decline, her parents took her out of public school and hired a private tutor for her. This personal attention gave her a great education but few social skills.

She was profoundly shy and awkward with people. Her parents tried to lift her sagging spirits by encouraging her interest in play-acting. They had no idea that this innocent family game would become her life's obsession. To her parent's great dismay, she chose to become an actress.

In college, Kathy took drama classes and appeared in school plays. After college, she went to New York to strike out on the stage. *Literally*. She suffered from stage fright and her voice was too high and tinny-sounding.

A lead role in the play, "Death Takes A Holiday," was offered to her. But three days before opening night the producer asked for her resignation. "Resign...!" Kathy fired back. "If he wants me out of the cast, he can fire me." He was more than happy to oblige her.

In a different production company, she had a similar run-in with a fellow actor. He shouted at her,

"You're a fool! You'll never be a star. You'll never be important in the theater. You don't make any sense at all."

Kathy didn't get intimidated easily. She yelled right back, "You're the fool! I will be a star before you're ever heard of!"

She was right. George Coulouris, an actor you've probably never heard of, was dead wrong. She might not always have made sense to other actors, but she made many dollars, thanks to her adoring fans. Although early on she earned a reputation as "box-office poison" because of her head-strong temperament, Kathy became a big box office draw.

Whether it was teaming up with Spencer Tracy in *Guess Who's Coming to Dinner,* or Humphrey Bogart in *The African Queen*, Kathy held her own. She won her first Academy Award in 1933, and has earned three other Oscars since then.

After her final performance in a Broadway musical many years ago, she summed up her success when she told the audience after a long standing ovation, "Well—I love you and you love me, and that's that." Yes, Katherine Hepburn, that pretty well sums it up.

Stand Up to Them!

**Anybody can tell you what "You'll never be!"
But only you can see what you will be.**

The World's Greatest Misprint

Have you ever heard of Thomas E. Dewey, the 34th President of the United States? No? That's odd. On the last weekend in October 1948, *Life* magazine put out its November 1st issue. It had a full-page photograph of Governor Dewey and his wife with the caption:

"The next President travels by ferry boat over the broad waters of San Francisco Bay."

Dewey, the governor of New York, was considered a shoo-in on election day. "I've finished my editorial congratulating the new President," bragged the editor in chief of the *Baltimore Sun*. "It's in type and on the stone." He was that confident of a Dewey victory. With a twinkle in his eye, he added, "If Truman won, I'd have to write another one, wouldn't I?"

Not one pollster predicted that Harry Truman, the sitting president, would win. No radio commentators or newspaper columnists, or any one of the hundreds of reporters who covered the campaign thought Truman had a prayer.

Near midnight on election day, an NBC political commentator mentioned that Truman was ahead by 1.2 million votes. Ignoring the growing evidence to the contrary, he added that Truman was still "undoubtedly beaten."

But the clincher was a banner headline in the *Chicago Tribune* on November 4, 1968 (the day after the election). It trumpeted:

DEWEY DEFEATS TRUMAN

But Truman beat Dewey by 2.2 million in the popular vote and had 114 more electoral votes. Granted, it was a narrow margin of victory in three key states. Truman won in Ohio by just 7,000 votes. In California, it was by 17,000 votes. In Illinois, the margin was

33,000. It was not a landslide, by any stretch. But that doesn't change the fact that Truman won and Dewey lost.

How could all the "experts" have been so wrong?

Comedian Fred Allen quipped, "Harry Truman was the first president to lose in a Gallup and win in a walk." Yes, the voters made fools of the experts. Some said "a great roar of laughter arose from the land." And the yolk was smeared on the face of the media's elites.

A great deal of soul-searching by the editors, the broadcasters, and the pollsters followed Truman's surprising victory. One wag took great delight in pointing out that the surprising outcome "shook the bones of all the smarties."

Congresswoman Clare Booth Luce was one of those who predicted that Truman was a "gone goose." She and all the other experts got their gooses cooked.

Stand Up to Them!

**When "they" can't possibly be wrong,
why are you so sure "they" are right?**

"I Wish I May, I Wish I Might..."

During a trip to Washington, D.C. in 1935, a young man wrote this in a letter to his wife:

> **"Honey, I can see how someday, if you and I just apply ourselves and make up our minds to work for bigger and better things, we can someday live here in Washington and probably be in government, politics, or service. . . . Oh, gosh, I hope my dream comes true—I'm going to try anyhow."**

Yes, indeed, you could say that he got involved in Washington politics and government. But young Hubert Humphrey never dared to imagine that he would run for President! But he did.

Stand Up to Them!

**Your biggest dreams
might not be big enough**

"Lasting" Results

You won't know his name. It won't ring a bell. But you are indebted to him to the bottom of your sole. He invented a machine that transformed an industry, helped launch a major corporation, created jobs for thousands of American workers, and made millions of dollars for several men. Unfortunately, he was not one of them.

This man's invention mechanized a procedure called "lasting," a process all the experts assumed would always be done by manual labor.

"Lasters" boasted that no machine could ever replace their delicate fingers fastening the body of the shoe to the inner sole.

Jan immigrated to Philadelphia when he was 21 years old. His timing was horrible. His adopted homeland was in the grip of a deep depression following the Panic of 1873. Eighteen thousand businesses went belly-up and half a million workers lost their jobs. Unable to speak the language, he had a tough time finding work as a skilled machinist.

In desperation, he apprenticed as a shoemaker and learned to operate a McKay sewing machine. It stitched the outer sole of a shoe to the inner sole. After two or three years in Philly, Jan heard about Lynn, Massachusetts, "the shoe capital of the world." It sounded like a natural fit, so he made the move.

It was in "the shoe capital" that Jan must have heard the conventional wisdom that "lasters" were irreplaceable. It took a skilled worker five or six minutes to "last" one shoe. This meant that a "laster" could only stitch fifty or sixty pairs of shoes a day. Shoe parts that were made by machine piled up, demanding his attention. "Lasters" were the bottleneck in shoe production. Somebody had to do something, and Jan did.

After working ten hour days in the factory, Jan retired to his own primitive shop to design, build, and patent a "lasting" machine. It could stitch several hundred pairs of shoes per day. He succeeded on one end, but failed on another.

In a hurry to sell his patents, he settled for approximately $15,000. Over the next fifteen years, his patents generated $50 million in business for one new shoe conglomerate alone. Shoes dropped in price by half while production soared.

Jan did not live to see the success of his invention. He died a few years after he sold his creation at age 36. His "lasting" machine outlasted him by many years. And, unfortunately, his accomplishments did not generate a lasting memory for his name.

But remember, this was a young man whose mother was a black plantation slave from the Dutch colony of Surinam. Jan Matzeliger did not live long. But he achieved "lasting" results.

Stand Up to Them!

**They may not remember your name,
but make them remember your claim to fame.**

Dive In With Both Feet

Laura broke her bones in the wrong place at the wrong time. She broke her foot in three places just a few months before the most important tryouts in her athletic career.

No one thought she would make the team.

Except Laura. She missed seven weeks of training. Then returned to practice with a cast on her foot. Her broken bones weren't healing properly, but she gutted it out. No pain, no gain. Those words weren't a cliché to her. They were a way of life. She survived the qualifying rounds and made the team.

Most analysts were convinced that the best Laura could hope to achieve was a sixth place finish.

But not Laura. She believed that she could win the competition. Every time Laura stepped up to the platform, she smiled and mumbled to herself. Fans wondered what she was saying, noticing her lips mouthing words every time she competed. Her style and grit made her a fan favorite.

In a dramatic come-from-behind finish, Laura achieved first place in the competition. Her face, reflecting the thrill of victory, would grace *Wheaties* boxes for months. She had done something no American athlete had been able to achieve in decades.

"It's been 36 years since the United States won a gold medal in platform diving," a reporter acknowledged. "Can you put your emotions in words?"

Sure she could. Laura Wilkinson chose the same words she had mumbled every time she stepped to the edge of the platform in the 2000 Olympic Games. She smiled and said,

"I can do all things through Christ who strengthens me."

Later she added, "God was with me."

No wonder fans adored her. She was playing to an audience of One.

Stand Up to Them!

**When you say, "I can do it!",
where does your strength come from?**

Epilogue

Elbert Hubbard was a wise man. Without the benefit of reading these stories, he came to the same conclusion that you did. Hubbard observed,

"The world is moving so fast these days that the man who says it can't be done is generally interrupted by someone doing it."

O.K. You have kept your end of the bargain. You have read these magnificent stories showing how courageous men and women dared to say, "YES I CAN! I can stand up to life's put-downs! I refuse to let people tell me `You can't!' and set my limits for me."

Did you find yourself saying, "YES I CAN!" too? If not, maybe you need to start over. Read these stories again and again until you can say, without a shred of doubt, "YES I CAN!"

Maybe you noticed that some of these gutsy people had to stand up to their own put-downs—meaning the limits they imposed on themselves. They triumphed because they rejected that earlier impulse to limit what they could accomplish. Or time and circumstances reversed the gloomy verdict they had rendered regarding their own potential success or failure.

For example, Abraham Lincoln concluded that he had embarrassed the American people with his "brief, pithy remarks" at Gettysburg. He thought that the speech was a failure. But time and the verdict of history have proven him wrong. It was his greatest speech, and perhaps the greatest speech in American history.

Think back to two of the other stories you read in this book.

- If Einstein's headmaster was wrong about young Albert, then maybe those who predicted that you will never amount to much are equally wrong.

- If Ray Kroc, the founder of McDonald's, was selling himself short when visions of milk shake machines danced in his head, then maybe you are selling yourself short, too.

You get the idea. Now put it to work.

Someone quipped regarding Columbus and his discovery of America,

When he set out, he didn't know where he was going.
When he got there, he didn't know where he was.
When he returned, he didn't know where he had been.

When you started this book, you might not have been sure where you were headed. But, now that you have finished it, you know where you've been. Plus, you have a better idea where you're headed and how to get there.

Great things are in store for you as long as you can ignore those nasty "Prophets in reverse." They view the future through a rear-view mirror. They guess-timate your future limitations based upon your past mistakes or failures. That is their mistake. Don't make the same mistake. That would be a big mistake.

Remember your past is only the prologue. It explains how you got where you are. But it does not demand that you stay there. Find the courage to write your own epilogue. Where you are going is more important than where you've been. Determine what you want etched on your tombstone and then chisel your life around your end game.

Refuse to stay down when you get put-down. Stand up to your critics! You can do it! You know you can. Say it with me:

YES I CAN!

Index

This is not an exhaustive index. It is designed to help you find the People, Places, and Subjects of importance mentioned in YES I CAN! It is intended to provide a quick reference to the stories you have read and enjoyed.

TWA 159
Twain, Mark 50, 55

U

"übergeek" 165-166
Uncle Tom's Cabin 29-31
Union Army 168
Union Pacific 114
United Nations 160
U.S. (see United States)
U.S. Navy 73
United States (U.S.) 8, 29, 54, 78-79, 86, 89-91, 102, 114-115, 123, 131-132, 150, 170, 177, 182
United States Patent and Trademark Office 75
United States Senator(s) 81, 89, 91
United Technologies Corp. 56
University of Minnesota 76
"unrepentant bachelor" 153-154
USA Today 73
Utah 133
Utica, NY 121

V

Van Buren, Martin – U.S. Pres. 54-55
Velpau, Dr. Alfred 96
Versailles 69
Vesti la giubba 36
Vietnam 164
Virginia 79
Voltaire 172

W

Wall Street 123, 125
Wall Street Journal, The 56, 58, 150
Wal-Mart 143-144
Walton, Sam 143-144
Washington Post, The 78, 127

Washington, Booker T. 78-80
Washington, D.C. 133, 179
Washington, George – U.S. Pres. 49
Watson, Thomas, Jr. 112
Watson, Thomas, Sr. 111-112
Webster, Daniel 81
wedding 146
West Virginia 137
Western roll and straddle 84
Western Union 115
Western Union Telegraph Co. 173-174
Wheaties 182
White House 37, 38, 71, 78-79
White Star Line 64
Whittier, John Greenleaf 30
Wilkinson, Laura 182-183
Williamsport, MD 88
Wilson, Grady 63
Wilson, Kemmons 148, 150-151
Wilson, Thomas Woodrow – U.S. Pres. 37, 130-131
Windows 111
Windows magazine 92
Windsor Castle 37
Winfrey, Oprah 10-11
Wonder, Stevie 98
Woolworth, Frank W. 120-122
World Series, the 158
World War II 132, 137
Wright Brothers 83
Wright, James 170-171

X

X-1 137-138
xerography 68
Xerox 68

Also Available from Kenneth J. Brown

Timely Insights could do for your soul what the Atkins Diet does for the body. It is low-carb reading with plenty of spiritual meat.

Each *Timeless Truth* is introduced by a story about Madonna or Walter Payton, or even some math teacher. They are quick and interesting, offering poignant thoughts that stick with you all day.

"Adrenaline for the heart and spirit!"

To order: Call toll free **866-669-4047**.   Retail price $15.95.

Ask for the *YES I CAN!* special.